Thanks for (
the Bar M

Yossi Deitsch שיחי׳

14 Sivan, 5774

Chabad of Midtown, Toronto
Rabbi Nechemia & Devora Deitsch

THE
CHASSIDIC
APPROACH
TO JOY

BY RABBI SHLOMA MAJESKI

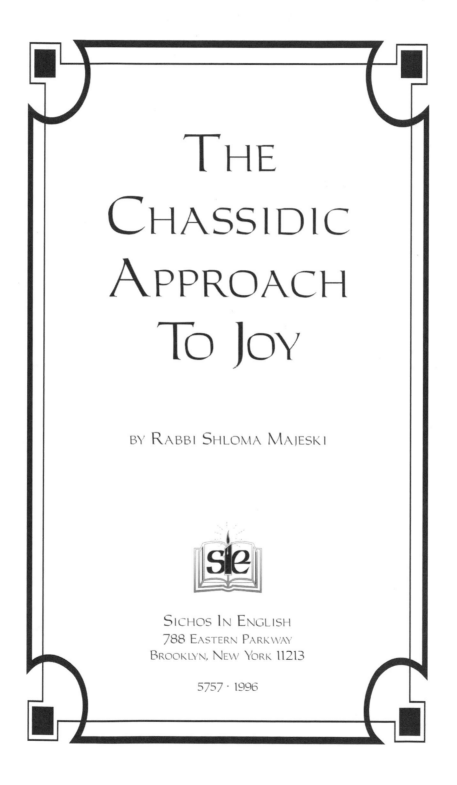

SICHOS IN ENGLISH
788 EASTERN PARKWAY
BROOKLYN, NEW YORK 11213

5757 · 1996

THE CHASSIDIC APPROACH TO JOY

Published and Copyrighted by
SICHOS IN ENGLISH
788 Eastern Parkway • Brooklyn, N.Y. 11213
Tel. (718) 778-5436

ISBN 1-8814-0012-3

First Printing 5755 • 1995
Second Printing 5757 • 1996

Table of Contents

Publisher's Foreword

Though one of the most sought after qualities, *simchah,* joy, is one of the easiest to acquire. Indeed, the very fact that a person feels difficulty is a sign that he is on the wrong path, for genuine happiness is an expression of inner truth and understanding, qualities that we all inherently possess. Nevertheless, sadness and depression incapacitate thousands of intelligent, capable individuals and drain the joy of life from many others.

What is at the core of this phenomenon? Why were certain individuals able to pull themselves together after the horrors of the Holocaust and build beautiful new lives, while others need only lose their car keys to find themselves in the midst of a crisis?

For more than two centuries, the mystical teachings of *Chassidism* have produced individuals who have been recognized for their joy and inspiration. Their radiant life and energy stems from their profound spiritual awareness and absolute clarity of direction. These are people who live for a purpose and derive vitality from it.

In my years as Principal of the Machon Chana Women's College in Crown Heights and in lecture tours throughout the country, I have observed the positive effects of extending the teachings of *Chassidism* to people with contemporary values and little or no Jewish background. With eagerness and enthusiasm, men and women from all walks of life have been able to apply these truths to their lives and begin their journey on the well-traveled path to pure, internal happiness.

This inspired me to prepare these lessons as audiotapes. The widespread interest in the tapes motivated me to communicate the same message in book form.

* * *

Although joy can be felt alone, happiness is enhanced by the presence of others. Indeed, the most exuberant celebration is experienced with other people. So too, this book reflects the fusion of many people's efforts. Thanks go to:

Dvorah Huntsman Klein and Ruth Pepperman for transcribing the tapes;

Eli Touger, for helping transform the content from a spoken form to a readable text;

Ira Jacobson and R.C. Schilder, who edited the text;

Yosef Yitzchok Turner for the layout and the typography; and

Rabbi Yonah Avtzon, Director of Sichos In English, whose assistance and encouragement at every phase made this project possible.

May the happiness we feel in the present age herald the ultimate rejoicing we will all experience with the coming of the Redemption — when Jews from all over the world will stream to *Eretz Yisrael,* our Holy Land, "crowned with eternal joy."[1]

* * *

The true source of inspiration to go out and spread the teachings of *Chassidus,* as well as the *Chassidic* concept of joy, is the Lubavitcher Rebbe himself, constantly urging, encouraging and inspiring all of us to share the beauty of *Chassidus* with all those within our reach.

Since the 3rd of the Hebrew month of Tammuz, when the passing of the Rebbe took place, many people have attempted to express their feelings about the Rebbe's greatness; however, they all arrive at the same conclusion, as in the words of *Akdomos,* "If all the trees were quills and all the oceans were ink, all the heavens were parchment and all the people were scribes," it would not be enough to express

1.   *Yeshayahu* 35:10, 51:11.

what we truly feel. The magnitude of the Rebbe's greatness and his accomplishments in absolutely every area of *Yiddishkeit* is totally beyond description.

Nevertheless, in regard to the subject of *simchah*/joy, we can certainly say that the Rebbe and the *Chassidic* concept of joy are absolutely one!

The Rebbe's approach to everything in life is with the emphasis on the positive and the emphasis on *simchah*. This is evident in all his talks, letters and his advice to people during *yechidus* (private audience).

The Rebbe himself personifies *simchah* and infuses all those around him with hope, vitality and joy.

When he walked into the shul, or out of the shul, it was always with a song of *simchah*. The *farbrengens* (*Chassidic* gatherings) were always full of joyous singing. Wherever the Rebbe went, with a wave of his hand, he encouraged joyous *Chassidic* song.

Whoever came in contact with him — the sick, the poor, the orphan, the widow, the lonely, the confused, or the simple pessimist — found that the Rebbe was aware of and understood their pain from their perspective. He always found the way, with just the right words, or with his smile, or a wave of his hand, to uplift, inspire and bring them all *simchah*.

In a talk given in the month of Elul during the year 5748 (1988), the Rebbe introduced *simchah* as the fundamental medium of action to bring about *Mashiach's* coming. This talk describes that connection between Redemption and *simchah* and was placed at the end of the book, because after considering the *Chassidic* view of joy, one will be able to better appreciate the Rebbe's talk.

The Rebbe has reiterated that our generation is certainly the last generation of exile and the first generation to experience Redemption. He publicized his prophecy that the coming of *Mashiach* is imminent, and what we must do now — he said — is to accept *Mashiach*. He declared that *Mashiach* is already here and revealed, that he has already begun to activate massive changes in the world (namely the process of reducing nuclear weapons and moving towards world peace), and stated openly that "his name is Menachem." We therefore express our hope that we merit immediately to see the Rebbe *Melech HaMashiach* once again in a physical body and he will lead us out of this exile and bring true unlimited joy to the Jewish people and the entire world.

Rabbi Shloma Majeski

Purim, 5755
Crown Heights, N.Y.

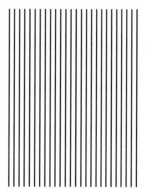

Chapter One
UNDERSTANDING, THE CORE OF JOY

Simchah, joy, is one of the most essential elements of the *chassidic* way of life. Indeed, in the early stages of the *Chassidic* movement, before the name *chassidim* was coined, one of the temporary names used to refer to *chassidim* was *di freilicha*, meaning, "the happy ones." How could you define and identify a *chassid*? By seeing if he was *b'simchah* — happy and joyous.

The Rebbeim, the leaders of the *Chassidic* movement, would always emphasize the importance of happiness and would urge their followers to strive to eradicate all traces of sadness and depression. R. Shlomo of Karlin would say that depression is considered the threshold of all evil. On another occasion, R. Shlomo said that although the 365 negative commandments do not include a commandment not to be depressed, the damage that sadness and depression can cause is worse than the damage that any sin can cause.

The Baal Shem Tov[1] would say that there are times, when the *yetzer hora* (the evil inclination) tries to persuade a

---

1.   *Tzavos HaRivosh,* ch. 44.

person to commit a sin, that it does not care whether or not the person will actually sin. What it wants is that after sinning, the person will become depressed and overcome with sadness. In other words, the depression that follows the sin can cause more spiritual damage than the actual sin itself.

The *Chassidic* emphasis on joy has its roots in the teachings of the *Kabbalah*. In that vein, the *AriZal* (see glossary) notes that the Torah[2] tells us that several harsh punishments will come "because you did not serve G-d with happiness and a glad heart." Other commentaries[3] explain that the intent of the verse is that the punishments will come because the people did not serve G-d in a time of pleasantness and joy. The *AriZal* explains,[4] however, that the verse should be understood simply. What is the reason for the punishments that will befall our people? Their Divine service lacked *simchah*; they lacked the vitality, energy, and connection to G-d that joy contributes to Divine service.

When a person is depressed or sad, his energy is drained; he becomes weak and it is possible that his evil inclination will overpower him. By analogy: If two people are wrestling each other, and one of them is stronger, he will be able to overpower the weaker one. If, however, the stronger person is depressed and lacks vitality, and the weaker person is full of energy, the weaker person will be able to overcome the stronger person.[5]

To refer back to the analogy: When a person is happy and full of energy, he can overcome his evil inclination. But even if he is spiritually strong, when a person is sad and his energy is drained, his *yetzer hora* can easily overcome him.

One might ask: Why are such teachings identified with *Chassidic* thought? Seemingly, these concepts would be accepted by people from all sectors of Jewish thought.

---

2. *Deuteronomy* 28:47.
3. *Rashi, loc. cit.*
4. See *Likkutei Sichos*, Vol. XX, p. 552.
5. See *Tanya*, Chapter 26.

Indeed, if they were extended slightly, they could be understood and accepted by secular thinkers as well. So why are they identified with *Chassidism?*

The answer[6] is that the theoretical basis that enables a person to translate these ideals from the abstract into the actual is inherent to *Chassidism. Chassidism* teaches that the vitality, and indeed the entire existence, of the world depends totally upon G-d. Every element of creation is one with G-d. Without this Divine energy, nothing could exist.

This leads to the appreciation of *hashgachah pratis,* Divine Providence. Everything that transpires, not only what happens to people, but also everything that happens to inanimate objects, comes as a direct result of G-d's will. Not only does every entity in the world exist by virtue of G-d's life-force; every event that occurs in the world takes place because G-d causes it to happen.[7]

The awareness of these concepts leads directly to *simchah.* For a person who is aware that everything that happens to him is controlled by G-d will surely be happy. Indeed, when a person lacks such happiness, he is implying, Heaven forbid, that what is happening is *not* connected to G-d, or that G-d is causing it to happen, but that, Heaven forbid, G-d is not good.

This is a direct denial of G-d. If one believes that G-d is responsible for everything that happens, and believes that G-d is good, then naturally everything that happens is good.

If a person got up and made a declaration that everything that happens does not come from G-d, he would be denying G-d's oneness. Even when one refrains from making such statements, but acts in a way that implies so — for example, if he is sad — the implication is the same.

---

6. See *Tanya, Iggeres HaKodesh,* Epistle 11.
7. See the essay entitled *Master Plan: The Baal Shem Tov's Unique Conception of Divine Providence* (Sichos In English, 5752).

Indeed, actions speak louder than words. So by being sad, a person is denying the oneness of G-d. He is denying the fact that everything in the world is constantly connected to G-d, and everything that happens is controlled by Divine Providence.

This is why *Chassidism*, which stresses so clearly and so powerfully the connection between the creation and G-d, places such an emphasis on *simchah*. In addition to the contribution of *simchah* to our Divine service — for as above, when a person is sad, he becomes weak and vulnerable, and his evil inclination can overpower him — something far larger than one's individual self is involved. Happiness and its opposite depend on whether or not one is aware of G-d's oneness and His constant providence.

In this context, we can understand a unique concept taught by our Sages. Our Sages state[8] that a person who loses his temper is considered as if he worshipped idols. What is the connection between losing one's temper and idol worship?

Losing one's temper is obviously undesirable. It reflects a lack of self-control; it is socially unacceptable; but how is it connected to idol worship? The answer is that when a person loses his temper, he, in essence, is denying that what has occurred is coming from G-d. If he believed that everything that happens comes from G-d, that G-d is good and whatever G-d does is good, there is no room for losing one's temper, just as there is no room for depression and sadness.

A person once came to R. Dov Ber, the Maggid of Mezeritch, and asked him, "Rebbe, our Sages tell us that we must bless G-d when something good happens, and in the same way, we should bless G-d when something negative happens.[9] How can this be actualized?"

---

8. *Zohar*, Vol. I, p. 27b, *Mishneh Torah, Hilchos De'os* 2:3; cf. *Nedarim* 22b. See also *Tanya, Iggeres HaKodesh*, Epistle 25.
9. *Berachos* 54a.

The Maggid of Mezeritch told him, "Go to my student, R. Zushya. He will explain it to you."

When he found R. Zushya, by looking at his face and his clothing he could easily see that he had not had much to eat, and that he did not have the money to buy decent clothing. Everything about him bespoke privation, but his face radiated happiness. "This is surely a person who can answer my question," he said to himself.

So he told R. Zushya that the Maggid had sent him to him to explain how a person could bless G-d in the face of adversity.

R. Zushya looked at him in puzzlement. "I do not know how to answer this question," he replied. "This question should be answered by someone who has suffered. I have never experienced suffering in my life."

R. Zushya was telling him that everything that happens comes from G-d and is controlled by Divine Providence. He knew clearly that G-d is completely good. Therefore, it was as clear as day to him that everything that happens is good. And so, R. Zushya never experienced any suffering in his life.

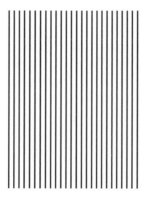

Chapter Two
BEING HAPPY AT ALL TIMES

Are the above concepts merely theories, or can we actually apply them to our lives? How can we come to terms with all the unpleasant things that happen, particularly if they are very painful, and they hurt. How can we say that everything that happens — even these painful things — is good, because it comes from G-d?

The Talmud tells us of two sages, Rabbi Akiva and his teacher, Nachum Ish Gamzu, whose conduct provides us with exemplary illustrations of how to resolve these questions. There was one phrase that Rabbi Akiva would continually repeat: *"Kol mah d'oveid Rachmono, l'tov oveid."* It means, "Everything that G-d does is for the good."[1]

Nachum Ish Gamzu had a similar phrase. He would say, *"Gam zu l'tovah,"* meaning "This is also for the good."[2] In fact, he would repeat this phrase so often that people called him Nachum Ish Gamzu, meaning, Nachum, the Gamzu man — the man who always says *gam zu l'tovah.*

---

1. *Berachos* 60b.
2. *Taanis* 21a. See also *Likkutei Sichos,* Vol. II, p. 393ff. which explains the contrasts between the paths of Divine service taught by these two Sages.

On the surface, it seems that they were both saying the same thing, just phrasing it in different words. But the truth is that the difference between them goes beyond semantics. Each had a different approach and a different level of perceiving how everything that happens comes from G-d and is good. The difference between them is reflected in the stories the Talmud tells us about each of these men, showing how their adages became translated into actual experience.

The Talmud tells us that once, while Rabbi Akiva was on a journey, he needed a place to spend the night. He knocked on the door of one of the homes in the town he was passing through, but the owner did not invite him in. He was not upset, for he realized, "Everything G-d does is for the good."

He knocked on another door, but again he was not offered hospitality. His reaction remained the same, "Everything G-d does is for the good." Even after he had gone from door to door and realized that no one in the town was going to accept him as a guest, he still said, "Everything G-d does is for the good."

He had no choice but to camp in a forest lying at the outskirts of the town. He was traveling with a donkey to carry his packages, a rooster to wake him up early, and a lamp with which he could study at night. Shortly after he encamped, a lion devoured his donkey, his rooster was killed by another predator, and a strong wind blew out his fire. After each of these events, Rabbi Akiva said, "Everything that happens is for the good."

And the Talmud continues, telling us that he was right. On the following morning, he discovered that during the night, a Roman legion had attacked this village and taken its people as captives. Had he been accepted as a guest in one of these homes, he too, would have been taken captive.

And if his donkey or rooster had been alive, their braying and crowing would have attracted the legionnaires' attention. Had his candle remained burning, they would have been able to see him in the forest. "Everything that happened was for the good."

The story of Nachum Ish Gamzu took place in the following setting: The Roman emperor had decreed a terrible decree against the Jews in *Eretz Yisroel*, and the Jews had sent Nachum Ish Gamzu as their representative to petition the emperor to annul the decree. They gave him a chest full of precious gems to present to the emperor as a gift in the hope of appeasing him.

On his way, Nachum Ish Gamzu stopped at an inn. The innkeeper realized that the Rabbi was carrying jewels in this chest. During the night, he and his family removed the gems and filled the chest with sand. When Nachum woke up in the morning and prepared to continue his journey, he realized the change in the chest's weight. Although he saw that the jewels had been stolen and exchanged for sand, he remained unfazed.

He said *gam zu l'tovah*, "this also is for the good," and continued to Rome. There he gained an audience with the emperor and presented him with the request of the Jewish people and their gift.

When the emperor opened the chest and saw the sand, he became enraged and ordered the Rabbi to be thrown into the dungeon. One of the king's advisors — actually, the Talmud teaches us, he was not really an advisor, but Elijah the Prophet in disguise — spoke up on the Rabbi's behalf.

"Do you think the Jews have lost their senses?" he asked the emperor. "They are coming to appease you and ask a favor. Why would they want to mock you? The Rabbi knows that he could be killed for bringing you sand.

"This cannot be ordinary sand. It must be something special. In the Jews' tradition, it says that their forefather Abraham used special sand to defeat his enemies. He fought against four strong kings. How was he able to vanquish them? He took sand and threw it into the air, and the sand turned into arrows and spears. Perhaps this is the same special sand."

The emperor was willing to experiment. The Romans were waging a war at that time, and they took the sand out to the battlefront. And the same miracle took place. They threw the sand in the air, and it became arrows and spears. Stunned and dismayed, the enemy was soon vanquished.

Needless to say, the emperor was very pleased with this news. He had Nachum Ish Gamzu taken out of the dungeon and thanked him for the wonderful gift that he had brought. He nullified the decree against the Jews, filled the chest that the Rabbi had brought with precious gems, and gave it to him as a present.

The two stories share a fundamental similarity. Both Rabbi Akiva and Nachum Ish Gamzu firmly believed that everything that happened was positive in nature. Even when confronted with adversity, they saw, in a very short period of time, that their belief was well-founded. Even the unfavorable circumstances in which they found themselves led to a positive outcome.

Nevertheless, if we look closely at these two stories, we can distinguish between the approaches of these two sages. Rabbi Akiva's statement, "Everything that G-d does is for the good," implies that since the situation is ordained by Divine Providence, G-d is behind it. Therefore, we can be sure that it will eventually lead to a favorable outcome.

In other words, the situation itself may be painful or unpleasant, but it will lead to a positive outcome. If we were to know the positive results from the outset, we would decide that it is worth enduring this negative experience for the sake of the positive experience. Rabbi Akiva taught that even when a person does not have such foreknowledge, he should have the faith that G-d is controlling his experience and should therefore accept everything with happiness.

To illustrate: Take a person undergoing a surgical operation: If a person who knows nothing about modern medicine would walk into the operating room, he would be terrified by the sight. A person is lying on a table with his hands and feet tied down. Someone with a mask on his face is standing over him with a knife in his hand, cutting away at his body.

It would not be surprising for such a person to scream "Murder!" But he would be screaming only because of his ignorance, because he does not see what the operation is leading to. He would respond differently if he knew that this is a process of healing which will improve the patient's health. Indeed, the patient is paying dearly for the surgery, and has waited weeks or even months for his turn to come.

What is the point of the analogy? Surgery is a painful experience; it is uncomfortable and unpleasant. But a person is willing to undergo such an experience because he believes the outcome will be so positive that it will have been worthwhile.

And this is the way Rabbi Akiva saw everything in life. He realized that everything comes from G-d. And so he believed that even the painful and negative experiences would eventually lead to something positive. These concepts were reflected in the story mentioned above. Rabbi Akiva confronted adversity. Yet, from the negative experience, good emerged. And indeed, the good was worth bearing the negative experiences which preceded it.

Nachum Ish Gamzu's approach was even deeper. He believed that since all situations were brought about by Divine Providence, not only would a situation that looked unfavorable eventually lead to a positive outcome, but that it was itself a positive event; "*This* is also for the good." To refer to the story mentioned previously, the exchange of gems for sand was a positive thing. Although at the time nobody realized that it was positive, Nachum Ish Gamzu had faith. And after a few days, everyone discovered how right he was.

The exchange worked far more effectively than anyone would have dreamed. Who knows whether the king would have been impressed by the precious gems and jewels? Precious stones would not have been anything new for him. The sand, by contrast, was definitely something that impressed the king and had a tremendous impact on him.

Why can't we, like Nachum Ish Gamzu, be happy in all situations? To put it bluntly, we are ignorant and unaware. We have not developed ourselves, and moreover, even the most developed person cannot have the same understanding as G-d. Therefore, we cannot always see or understand that a situation is good.

Let us take another example: a mother who is feeding her child. A person walking by the house might hear screaming and shouting; the child is hysterical. The passerby peeks in through the window and sees the mother standing next to the child. She has a spoonful of food and is trying to feed him.

What would you say? Is the mother doing something negative that will eventually lead to something positive, or is what she is doing positive now? We do not need any time to ponder the answer; indeed, the very question is hard to conceive. The mother is doing something very positive. She is contributing to the health, growth and development of her child.

Why is the child crying? Because he is an infant, and he does not understand that what his mother is doing is for his benefit. He just feels uncomfortable with this big spoon sticking in his mouth and food pouring all over the place. Because of his lack of awareness, even though his mother is doing something for his benefit, he cries loudly.

A child may be, after all, only about twenty or so years younger than his mother, and the difference between their levels of understanding is measurable. Nevertheless, the child can suffer from a lack of awareness that prevents him from understanding that what his mother is doing is good for him.

How much more so does this apply with regard to G-d, who is infinite? Indeed, when we are speaking about G-d, even the term "infinite" is not a sufficient description. Is it, therefore, any wonder that we cannot always understand what G-d is doing, why He is doing it, and that what He is doing is actually good? The difficulty, however, is merely a product of our limited understanding; in truth, everything that He does is good.

Since Divine Providence is controlling everything, a person should never see himself as a victim of circumstance. Whatever happens to him is ordained by G-d for a purpose, one that is ultimately for the person's own good. It is just that there are two kinds of good: goodness that is openly apparent, and goodness that is disguised and requires a frame of mind like that of Nachum Ish Gamzu or Rabbi Akiva to appreciate it.

We each encounter situations that are upsetting, and yet shortly afterwards we see that things work out for the best. How many times has it happened that a person missed his appointment, but because he missed the appointment, he was saved from a unfavorable investment, or was free to use his time differently and discovered a very positive opportunity.

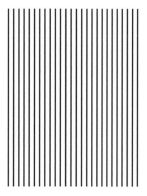

Chapter Three
SEEING THE SILVER LINING

Previously, we laid the foundations for the conception that everything that happens is for the good, postulating that this is so because everything that happens is governed by Divine Providence. Nothing happens merely as a quirk of nature; if G-d does not want it to occur, it cannot take place.

Moreover, G-d's will is purpose-oriented. Accordingly, since G-d is the epitome of goodness, everything that happens has a positive purpose. The more we understand the connection between G-d and our world — how they are really one — and the more we understand how G-d controls every event that occurs, the more we can understand how everything is ultimately good.

There are, however, certain things that happen in life that we cannot conceive of as being good. We try to adopt a new perspective, to look from this angle, or from that vantage point, and still these things do not appear good. In the story of Rabbi Akiva or in the story of Nachum Ish Gamzu, it took a day or several days for everyone to see how what happened was for the good. But there are certain times when you just cannot make the connection. In fact, sometimes, we see a person perform a good deed or act pleasantly, and yet a short while later, he is forced to suffer because of it.

How can this be explained? One of the classic explanations can be derived from a story from the *Midrash*,[1] which describes a journey that one of the Sages, Rabbi Yehoshua ben Levi, shared with Eliyahu *HaNovi*, Elijah the Prophet.

Once, when Rabbi Yehoshua encountered Eliyahu *HaNovi*, he asked Eliyahu if he could accompany him so that he could learn from his conduct. Eliyahu refused, explaining that Rabbi Yehoshua would not understand what he would see. On the contrary, his mortal mind would raise countless questions and there would be no time for explanations.

Rabbi Yehoshua ben Levi nevertheless begged and pleaded; he promised that he would not ask any questions. Eliyahu finally agreed on the condition that as soon as Rabbi Yehoshua would begin to ask questions, they would part company.

And so they set out together. Toward evening, they reached an old, shaky hut. An elderly couple was sitting outside. While their features bespoke a dimension of dignity, they were obviously poor. But their poverty did not hamper their enthusiasm to welcome guests. As soon as they saw the travelers, they jumped up and eagerly invited them into their home, offering them a meal and a place to sleep.

Admittedly, the accommodations were somewhat lacking because the people did not have very much. But whatever they had, they were willing to share, doing the best they could to observe the *mitzvah* of *hachnosas orchim*, showing hospitality to guests.

The following morning, the two travelers bade their hosts farewell and set out again. Shortly after they had departed, Rabbi Yehoshua ben Levi saw that Eliyahu *HaNovi* was praying. He listened closely. What was Eliyahu praying

---

1. *Seder HaDoros, Erech* R. Yehoshua ben Levi, sec. 4 (p. 192).

for? The elderly couple who had hosted them owned a cow. The cow was the most valuable possession they owned — indeed, the majority of their income came from the cow's milk. Eliyahu was praying that this cow should die.

When Rabbi Yehoshua heard this, he was shocked. The couple had been so nice, so pleasant, so warm. Why did they deserve that their cow should die? But he could not ask any questions; that was the agreement he had made.

As they proceeded on their journey, they talked. Rabbi Yehoshua hoped that Eliyahu would offer an explanation for what happened, or at least a hint in that direction. But that was not so; instead he directed the conversation to other issues. Toward evening, they came to a beautiful mansion. Although many members of the household saw them, no one offered them hospitality.

They asked the owner of the house, a very rich man, for permission to spend the night in his home. Reluctantly, the man agreed. But he was very cold to them; he did not offer them any food, and he hardly said a word to them.

After they set off on their way in the morning, Rabbi Yehoshua noticed that Eliyahu was praying again. What was he praying for this time? One of the walls in this rich man's house was cracked and weak. Eliyahu was praying to G-d that this wall should be restored and should remain strong and solid.

Rabbi Yehoshua could not understand this. Here the person was a miser, who had not acted kindly to them at all. And yet Eliyahu was praying for him, entreating G-d that his wall, which was cracked, should become solid and strong again. But once more, he abided by the terms of his agreement: no questions allowed.

Eventually, the two travelers arrived in a beautiful city; everything about the place reflected prosperity and opulence. They made their way to the *shul*. It was a magnificent structure, designed with elegance and taste. Everything, even the benches, was beautiful.

Rabbi Yehoshua ben Levi thought that they would have no problem receiving hospitality in such a town. But it did not work out that way. The people were not very kind. When the prayers were over, nobody approached them to ask where they planned to eat or where they planned to stay. Ultimately, they had to spend the night in the *shul*, sleeping on those beautiful benches, without eating supper.

In the morning, when they were ready to leave, Eliyahu blessed the inhabitants of the city, wishing them that they should all become leaders. Again, Rabbi Yehoshua was puzzled. Why did Eliyahu bless people who had not shown them hospitality?

That evening, they came to another city. Obviously, it was not as wealthy a community as the first; the *shul* was nowhere near as beautiful. But the people were very fine, warm and kind. They did everything they could to make the two travelers comfortable. Before leaving that city, Eliyahu told them, "May G-d help that only one of you becomes a leader."

At this point, Rabbi Yehoshua could no longer contain his curiosity. He told Eliyahu, "I know that by asking questions I will forfeit my right to accompany you, but I cannot go on like this. Please, explain these four incidents to me."

And so Eliyahu began to explain: "The elderly couple whom we met first; they were wonderful people who performed acts of great kindness. So I wanted to give them a blessing. It was destined for the woman to pass away that day; it was to be the last day of her life.

"But by hosting us, she was given the opportunity to perform a *mitzvah*. And the merit of the *mitzvah* of hospitality that she performed was great enough for the decree to be lifted, but not entirely. So I prayed that their cow — which meant so much to them and which was their source of income — should die. Because the cow would die, the woman would have many more years to live. So the cow's death was really a blessing for them.

"About the miser's house. In that wall, a very great treasure lay buried. But the wall was weak and would soon break. Because he was a miser and conducted himself so crudely, I prayed that the wall should become strong so that he would not be able to benefit from the treasure.

"What about the people in the prosperous city?" Eliyahu continued. "My prayer that they should all become leaders in the city is not a blessing; if anything, it is the opposite. For the most destructive thing that can happen in a city is that everybody becomes a leader.

"In the other city, where the people were kind, I gave them a genuine blessing: that one, and only one, of them become a true leader."

This story contains a lesson for all of us. Like Rabbi Yehoshua ben Levi, we have to realize that life is a large puzzle with many pieces, of which we possess only a small portion. So, of course, we have questions. It is natural. For what we know about ourselves and about others is only a few pieces of a 5,000-piece puzzle. Is it any wonder that these few pieces do not seem to mean anything? The form of these pieces, the shape that results from their combination, does not look like anything, nor does it appear to lead to anything.

But that is because we have only a few pieces of a 5,000-piece puzzle. Once we receive the other four-thousand nine-hundred odd pieces and we add these few, everything falls into place and we see exactly how it fits in.

So we have to be patient and realize that we do not have the whole picture. Not about ourselves, about what happened before in our lives, what will happen later in our lives, about others in our community, or even about our parents and our children. And therefore, our vision is very limited, and we do not understand many of the things we see.

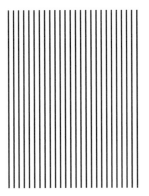

Chapter Four
EXPANDING OUR HORIZONS

As explained in the previous chapter, expanding our scope of vision opens us up to the possibility that there are processes of causation at work within the world of which we are unaware. There are questions, however, that remain unanswered. What about a person who is, G-d forbid, ill for life? Or, G-d forbid, a person to whom an accident occurs, causing his life to end. What can be said in such a case? How can we say that this is leading to something good?

The answer is that if one believes only in this physical world, the question will remain a question. But ours is not the only framework of existence. A true appreciation of reality extends far beyond the world that we see with our physical eyes.

Firstly, there is an afterlife, *Olam HaBo*, the World to Come. *Olam HaBo* is the world of the souls; after a soul leaves the body, it ascends to this spiritual world. But this is not the end of the soul's journey.

Ultimately, the soul will descend again, return to this physical world, and go back into its original body. For one of the Thirteen Principles of Faith[1] is that in the Era of the Redemption, the dead will be resurrected.[2] And so the soul's life does not end in our material world. On the contrary, it will live eternally in *Olam HaBo* and in the end of days be resurrected again in this world.

This knowledge expands our vision even further, and gives us a new vantage point with which to appreciate any suffering that we experience in our lives. It is true that in this life a person may suffer, but in *Olam HaBo*, in the life of the soul, he will reap the reward and the good that is to come from such suffering.

Indeed, the *Ramban*, in his commentary on the Book of *Iyov* (Job),[3] states that even if a person were to suffer, G-d forbid, like Job for a period of 70 years, this would be insignificant compared to even a brief period of suffering that the soul feels in *Gehinnom*.

Gehinnom refers to the spiritual realm in which the soul undergoes a period of cleansing and correction after it leaves our material world. In some texts, this process of cleansing and correction is referred to as punishment. The term is somewhat misleading, for the intent is not, Heaven forbid, to punish; we are speaking about a process of refinement and correction. But it is a painful process, far greater than any pain of which we can conceive. As we said, seventy consecutive years of Job's suffering in our material world is insignificant when compared with one moment of suffering in *Gehinnom*.

---

1. *Rambam's Commentary on the Mishnah,* Introduction to the Tenth Chapter of *Sanhedrin.* An abbreviated form of these thirteen principles (each beginning *Ani Ma'amin*) is printed at the end of the morning prayers in many *siddurim.*

2. See the comments of the *Ramban* in *Shaar HaGmul,* where he explains that the Era of the Resurrection will represent the ultimate reward of the soul, surpassing even the reward it receives in *Olam HaBo.*

3. See the explanation of this concept in *Tanya, Iggeres HaTeshuvah,* chapter 12.

(The same is true regarding pleasure. All the pleasure a person can experience in this world is insignificant compared with one moment of pleasure in the World to Come.[4])

In His kindness, G-d allows the suffering that we experience in this world to take the place of suffering in *Gehinnom.* An analogy to this is the motion of the sun. In space, the sun is moving millions of miles per hour, but in that time, the shadow cast by the sun on a wall may move only an inch or two. One inch of motion here is equivalent to millions of miles of motion there.[5]

In a similar way, one moment of suffering in this physical world will make up for far more intense suffering in the World to Come. And in that sense, all the suffering that a person endures in this world is ultimately for the good. While living in this physical world we may be unaware of this, but ultimately we will appreciate this reality in the World to Come or in the Era of the Redemption.

When we are aware of this concept, it changes the way we look at life around us. Once, the previous Lubavitcher Rebbe was arrested in Russia for spreading Jewish practice. The people who arrested the Rebbe were also Jewish; they belonged to the Jewish wing of the Communist party known as the *Yevseksia.* Perhaps it was their Jewish origin that motivated them to cruelly and ruthlessly try to stamp out Jewish observance. They demanded that the Rebbe give them information concerning the network of underground *yeshivas* and *chadarim* that he had established, to tell them about the location of kosher slaughterhouses, *mikvaos,* and so on. The Previous Rebbe was not intimidated and refused to give any information.

Finally, his interrogator took out a gun and pointed it at the Rebbe, saying, "Do you see this little toy? This little toy has made a lot of people talk; it will make you talk as well."

---

4.   *Pirkei Avos* 4:17.
5.   See *Tanya, loc. cit.*

The Rebbe answered very firmly, "That toy can only frighten people who have one world and many gods. A person who has one G-d and two worlds is not afraid of your little toy."

What the Previous Rebbe meant was that those people who are aware of absolute truth and are concerned with two worlds — this physical world, and also the spiritual world to come — are not frightened by the possibility of physical death. For this is not where life ends. And thus, what appears as a tragedy in this world may prove to be for the best in an ultimate sense.

In a limited sense, this concept can be accepted easily. But many will protest against extending it without bounds. Take the Holocaust, for example. Is there any way in which the cruel death of six million Jews can be explained as being for the good?

The truth is, we cannot explain how tragedies like these are for the good. On the contrary, any explanations or rationales man might offer seem vulgar and crass. For no man can set himself up as G-d and dictate reasons why another person should live or die.

But we must realize that our inability to understand and provide reasons does not alter the fact that the Holocaust and other bitter events that have taken place in our world, and indeed, everything that takes place in this world, even the fluttering of a leaf in the wind, is controlled by Divine Providence. And if the event is controlled by Divine Providence, G-d surely has His reasons. We cannot understand His reasons, for He and His wisdom are infinite, but our lack of ability to comprehend these reasons does not detract from their existence.

The difference between G-d and a human being is the difference between the finite and the infinite. There is no way we can expect to understand and comprehend events that reflect G-d's infinity. To illustrate the concept with a gross physical comparison: If a person went outside at night, looked up at the sky, and said, "There is nothing on the moon because I cannot see it," or "there is nothing beyond the moon because I cannot see it," everyone would laugh at him.

Now, why can he not see it? Because the moon, the planets, and the stars are millions of miles away, and we cannot see anything that far away. Some stars are not only millions of miles away — they are light years away. So even if we know they exist, we cannot know anything about what happens on them.

Nevertheless, all physical space, even at a distance of hundreds of light years, is a finite distance. When we speak about our distance from G-d, or His wisdom, we are talking about an infinite distance. And so, if with regard to physical things we are prepared to accept the idea that things exist even though we do not see them, so too, we should be willing to accept that G-d has reasons for everything that takes place, even when we cannot appreciate those reasons with our mortal minds. There is no way in the world we can fathom a possible explanation of the good stemming from events like the Holocaust, because our limited minds cannot comprehend something that is infinitely removed from them. But there is no way that G-d will allow something to happen that is not for the good.

There is, nevertheless, another point that has to be clarified. If a person suffered as a result of an act of G-d, Heaven forbid — be it a thunderstorm, an earthquake, or a disease — we can appreciate that in it there is hidden good. That is implied by the very name "an act of G-d." But when a loss is inflicted on a person by another individual — for example, an act of violence or a robbery — how can we say that it is, in essence, good? Why compare it to an act of G-d? On the contrary, the other person had free choice whether to commit the wrong or not.

Seemingly, the person who suffers is a victim of the other person's harmful impulses. On the surface, had the other person not chosen to do him harm, he would not have suffered this loss. How then can we say that this loss is in essence good because it is coming from G-d, when it is another human being who is responsible for it?

The resolution is, once again, that everything that happens is ordained by Divine Providence. Even when the loss is inflicted by another individual, it never would have happened[6] had it not been destined for the person to suffer this loss. Although the person who perpetrated the wrong chose to do so independently, the person who suffered, did so because he was destined to. Had this not been his destiny, the person who perpetrated the wrong would never have been able to do so. For example, when a thief chooses to steal from another person, the victim was destined to lose the money. Had the thief not chosen to steal, the victim would have lost the money some other way.

(This does not release the thief from the responsibility for his deed. Although the person was destined to lose his money, G-d has many emissaries at His disposal.[7] The thief knows nothing of G-d's plan. He stole because he chose to do evil, and he will therefore be punished.

The *Mishnah*[8] tells us that Hillel once saw a skull floating on the water. He said to it, "Because you drowned others, you were drowned; and ultimately, those who drowned you will themselves be drowned." Hillel was explaining the process of causation. The person made a wrong choice and drowned others. Since G-d punishes "measure for measure,"[9] drowning leads to drowning. In each instance, the person who was drowned received that punishment for a reason. Nevertheless, the person who served as the medium

---

6. See *Tanya, Iggeres HaKodesh,* Epistle 25, where the concepts mentioned here are explained in depth.
7. *Zohar* III, 36b.
8. *Pirkei Avos* 2:6.
9. *Nedarim* 32a.

to administer that punishment did so of his own volition, and hence he is punished for that choice.)

Therefore, the fact that one suffers a loss that is caused by another person should not prevent one from being *b'simchah* (happy). On the contrary, he should recognize that this loss was destined by G-d, and thus is, in essence, good.

For these reasons, a person should always be *b'simchah*, because everything that happens to him is coming from G-d, and G-d is good. And so, everything that happens is in essence good. Sometimes, the good and the blessing G-d bestows can be perceived openly. At other times, the good is disguised and cannot be seen immediately. But even these things are in essence good.

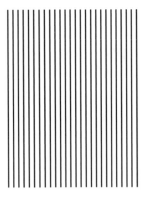

Chapter Five
PROBING BENEATH THE SURFACE

Up until now, we have endeavored to explain that a person should always be happy because everything that occurs to him is good. The only difference is whether that good is openly perceived, or that good is disguised. This thesis itself, however, requires explanation. Why does G-d sometimes give good in a disguised way? What is the purpose behind this?

A story is told about the Maggid of Mezeritch. Once, his son came running to him in tears. The Maggid comforted him and asked him why he was crying. The child began to explain that he had been playing a game of hide-and-go-seek with his friends.

He and all his friends were hiding. They remained in their hiding places for a long time, thinking that they had hidden themselves well, and the person who was "it" was unable to find them. But soon they got tired of waiting. They came out of their hiding places and found out that they had been wrong. The one who was "it" was not even there. He had played a trick on them. After they went into their hiding places, he went home instead of searching for them. That is why the Maggid's son and his friends were crying.

When the Maggid of Mezeritch heard this story, he also began to cry. His son asked him why he was crying. The Maggid told him that G-d has the same complaint.

What did the Maggid mean? It is written,[1] "You are a G-d who hides." G-d says, "I hide Myself from you, but the purpose of My hiding is that you should come and search for Me. But instead of searching for Me, you go away and busy yourselves with other things."

To apply the concept to the question at hand: When a negative thing happens and a person feels broken, the reason he feels broken is not the negative event itself. As explained above, many people have suffered difficulty without being broken. The person is broken because he does not recognize that G-d is hiding, and that the purpose of this negative event is to motivate him to search and find G-d, even as He is hidden. If the person only realized that, he would not be broken.

To employ an analogy: A father wishes to see how clever his child is. He wants to bring out and develop the intelligence of the child, and with that intent in mind, he hides from the child. If the child is very young, he immediately begins to cry because he cannot find his father. A child who is more mature thinks about what is happening and realizes that his father is playing with him. He therefore begins searching for his father until he finds him.

The purpose of the father's hiding is not to stay away from his child. On the contrary, he wants to be discovered, he wants the child to find him. But he wants the child to make the effort of looking for him and discovering where he is hiding.

---

1.   *Isaiah* 45:15.

The same applies regarding the analogy. The reason G-d disguises Himself and hides Himself is that He wants us to search for Him and find Him in the disguise, to probe deeply until we find where He is hiding.

And this analogy teaches us another powerful concept:[2] Not only is *simchah* important because it reflects the truth. When a person is *b'simchah*, this, itself, causes the disguise to be abandoned and prompts the good and the blessing to emerge to the surface.

Why? To refer back to the analogy, when the child continues searching for his father and finds where he is hiding, what happens then?

Does the father continue to hide? No. Once his son finds him, it is all over and he comes out of his hiding place. He had wanted his son to look for him, but once he finds him, he has no reason to continue hiding.

The same applies in regard to G-d and Jews. The purpose of G-d's hiding and His being disguised is that we should search for Him and learn to find Him. When a person is *b'simchah*, he is aware of G-d; it is as if he is saying, "Yes, G-d is hiding, but I can recognize and identify Him in these events even though He is hidden."

And then the mask is lifted and G-d emerges from hiding. Or to say it in different words, then the blessing and the goodness come to the surface.

This is the tremendous quality *simchah* possesses, that it causes the good to come out in the open. That is the unique virtue displayed by Rabbi Akiva and Nachum Ish Gamzu. Because these people saw very clearly that everything that happens comes from G-d, they knew that everything is definitely good. Therefore, they were always *b'simchah*.

And shortly thereafter, the difficulty that confronted them was transformed. The inner blessing and good that

---

2. See *Tanya, Iggeres HaKodesh*, Epistle 11.

was hidden was revealed. Because they recognized G-d, and sensed the goodness hidden in the disguise, the disguise was quickly dropped and the inner goodness surfaced.

A question, nevertheless, remains: Why does G-d disguise Himself? Why does He want us to search for Him? In the case of a father and his child, we can see the game as a form of entertainment. The father wants the child to look for him, so that the child will show how clever he is. Such a rationale is acceptable for human beings.

In our relationship with G-d, however, there must be a far deeper reason why G-d hides Himself, and why He desires that we search for Him. Why then does He hide? Surely there must be a positive purpose for His concealment.

∞

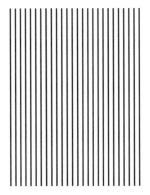

Chapter Six
CONFRONTING CHALLENGES

We explained previously that a person should always be happy because everything that happens to him, even difficulties and undesirable events, is controlled by Divine Providence. Therefore, a person should always be *b'simchah*, trusting that there is a positive, Divine intent in every aspect of his life.

We can accept this explanation with regard to difficulties on the material plane. When something unpleasant happens to a person, we can understand that it is disguised good. But what about events that are spiritually undesirable, that affect a person's soul as well as his body, something that stands in the way of a person's observing a *mitzvah*, or something that holds back a person's spiritual growth? How can we say that this is really good if it runs contrary to the Torah and its *mitzvos?* How can we say that this is controlled by Divine Providence when it is against G-d's will? On the surface, it cannot be good, for it conflicts with the Torah and prevents a person from advancing spiritually.

The resolution of this difficulty involves many profound questions in Jewish thought. The germ of the answer is the principle stated previously — that everything that takes places occurs only because G-d causes it to happen. Nothing takes place independently; nature has absolutely no independent power.

Every entity exists by virtue of the Divine energy invested in it. Every event that takes place — even one that appears negative — has a source in holiness. Otherwise, it could not exist. Therefore, even experiences that appear undesirable from a spiritual perspective must be appreciated as disguised good.

To explain: Something that appears to interfere with a person's spiritual growth and prevents the person from doing good is called a *nisayon,* a test. G-d is testing the person to see how committed he is to the Torah and its *mitzvos;* as it is written,[1] "And G-d, your L-rd, is testing you to know if you love G-d, your L-rd, with all your heart and all your soul."

Even when a person feels a challenge to his observance, he should realize that G-d is behind it. He is responsible for its happening, and through this challenge He desires to test the person.

What is the purpose of this test? On the surface, it appears that the purpose is that G-d wants to see how loyal and how committed the person is. But this explanation alone is not sufficient. When we are speaking about relations with other people, one person does not know what is going on in another person's heart or what is going on in his mind. Therefore, if he wants to know how committed the other person is, he must experiment. He has no choice.

For example, if one person wants to know whether another has true love, he has to set up certain circumstances and test how the other person will respond under these circumstances. He has no other way of verifying what is going on in the other person's heart and mind. But we cannot say

1. *Deuteronomy* 13:4.

such a thing about G-d. One of the basic principles of belief is that G-d knows what is going on in every person's mind and what is going on in every person's heart.

So why does He need to test us? Without subjecting us to a test, He can look into our hearts and minds and know how committed we are. Before the test begins, He knows whether we will be able to pass the test, or whether, Heaven forbid, we will not be able to past the test.

There are some commentaries[2] that explain that the purpose of the test is not for G-d to verify the person's commitment, but rather for the person to know himself. Sometimes, a person might not realize the strength of his commitment. So G-d puts the person to a test, and when the person is able to overcome the challenge, he reaches a more realistic awareness of his potential; he knows that his commitment is strong.[3] Thus, the purpose of the challenges a person faces is for his own knowledge, not for G-d's.

Chassidus provides a deeper explanation for the purpose of these tests and challenges, one that enables us to appreciate the G-dliness contained in these challenging experiences and prompts us to the awareness that they are in essence hidden good. It explains that the word *l'nasos,* which means "to test," also means "to raise high." The tests and challenges we face are intended to enable us to reach a higher spiritual level. Indeed, the way G-d chooses to enable the person to reach this higher spiritual level is through such tests and challenges.

Why is this? A person has two dimensions to his personality: a revealed dimension — i.e., the aspects of his personality that he usually expresses — and a hidden dimension, inner powers that do not always come to the

---

2.   See *Likkutei Sichos,* Vol. 20, p. 285, fn. 35 and sources cited there, *Derech Mitzvosecha* p. 370.

3.   We can also appreciate that failure can also serve a purpose, for it dashes a person's feelings of false pride and makes him realize the need for growth and development.

surface. These inner powers possess hidden resources of great strength.

We see this concept expressed in physical terms. Everyone has a magnitude of weight that he can lift under ordinary circumstances. Some people can lift 50 pounds easily; others can lift 100 pounds, and still others can lift 200.

There are times, however, when these ordinary limits are of no significance. We see that in an emergency — a fire, a flood, or the like — a person will jump great distances, bend bars, lift weights, and do other things that would be impossible for him to do under ordinary circumstances.

A story is told of a man who was repairing his car. He had lifted the car on a jack and his little daughter was sitting next to him with one foot underneath the car. The jack snapped and the car fell on her foot. With one hand, my friend lifted the car, and with the other hand, he gently pulled his daughter out from beneath the car. Afterwards, he rushed her to the hospital; all she needed was a cast.

Later, when he calmed down, he was quite puzzled. How was he able to lift the car? He tried to lift the car with both hands. Even with both hands, he was not able to lift it as high as he had previously been able with one hand. In biology, there is an explanation for this phenomenon. When we feel an emergency, the hormone adrenaline is released into the bloodstream, and this enables us to show far greater strength than usual.

Is this extraordinary strength created during the time of the emergency or is it there all the time? The answer is that it is there all the time. But until an emergency, it remains concealed. It does not surface in ordinary circumstances. When does it surface? When a person feels danger or challenge.

A parallel also exists on the level of emotion. A mother, for example, has tremendous love for her child. What would happen if, G-d forbid, that child would be kidnapped? Besides the fact that the mother would do everything within her power to find the child and to get him back, the mother would experience far greater feelings of love and yearning for her child than she does under ordinary circumstances.

Does this mean that the kidnapping of the child generated new feelings of love? Of course not. The love the mother feels always existed, but under ordinary circumstances deep love of this nature does not surface. Because her relationship with her child is being threatened and challenged, this deeper and more powerful feeling of love comes to the surface.

Indeed, this is the only way a love of this nature will be expressed. Under ordinary circumstances, no matter how much the mother would try, she would not experience such powerful feelings of love.

We also find a parallel on the level of intellect. For example, when a person studies, he comprehends the material according to his capacity. There are times when a person's mind is challenged; he is confronted with questions and difficulties, and this arouses a deeper level of understanding.

In this context, we can understand a famous statement of the Talmud,[4] "I received a lot from my teachers; I received even more from my colleagues. And from my students, I gained more than from anyone else." The students would challenge their teacher with questions. These questions would force the teacher to conceive of the subject in a different way than usual (for the students' minds worked differently than his did). By struggling to find a framework of reference with which to explain the concept to them, he penetrated to a deeper and more complete understanding of the idea himself.

We see a similar pattern in all three examples. Under ordinary circumstances, what surfaces is the external, superficial dimension of one's personality. And the only

4.   *Taanis* 7a.

thing that will get that deeper dimension to surface is a challenge.[5]

This is the purpose of a test. When a person serves G-d under ordinary circumstances, he develops a love for Him, but the love is limited, reflecting only the external dimensions of his personality. Every one of us contains a potential for much deeper love. But that deeper love does not surface under ordinary circumstances. It is only a challenge to a person's commitment to G-d that can spur this deeper dimension of love to surface.

When a person experiences a challenge in his observance of the *mitzvos*, or something happens that appears to hold him back from the study of the Torah, two things are happening simultaneously. On one hand, his relationship with G-d is being confined. Nevertheless, the inner motivation for this challenge is G-d's desire for the person to experience a deeper dimension of love, for him to be elevated to a higher rung. For as mentioned, the word *l'nasos* "to test" in Hebrew also means "to raise high."

This conception also enables us to understand a thought-provoking statement of our Sages,[6] "In the place that a *baal teshuvah* (a person who repents and returns to G-d) stands, a perfect *tzaddik* (righteous man) is incapable of standing."

How can a *baal teshuvah* stand on a higher level than a *tzaddik*? A *tzaddik* is a person who never sinned in his life. His life has been very pure; throughout his lifetime he has been striving upward, going from good to better.

The *baal teshuvah*, by contrast, has overcome his evil inclination, and at present is an example of good. But what about his past? His life had been tainted by sin. After he turns to G-d in *teshuvah*, G-d erases all those sins; it is as if they had never existed. But how can we say that this person

---

5.   See *Sefer HaMaamarim 5666*, p. 78ff.
6.   *Berachos* 34b.

stands higher than the *tzaddik*, a person who has devoted his entire life to personal development?

The answer is that a *tzaddik* never faced the challenges that a *baal teshuvah* confronts. A *tzaddik* is always serving G-d and has never felt distanced from Him. His love for G-d has become ingrained into his nature and part of his personality.

Although this is a great achievement, it reflects a certain limitation, for the powers of all mortals have certain bounds. When, by contrast, a person who feels cut off from G-d and very distant from Him labors to establish a bond with Him, he will experience far greater feelings of love than a *tzaddik* could possibly experience.

Why? Because he is confronting an inner challenge. He senses that he is separate from G-d, and must strive to reestablish his connection. Through these efforts, he activates the deeper dimension of love that every Jew possesses within his heart.[7]

We see a parallel in many situations. When a person undergoes a negative experience, it makes him appreciate the positive much more. In fact, it is impossible to have that same sense of appreciation without having first undergone the negative experience. For example, if a person, G-d forbid, lost his eyesight for two or three years and then regained it, he will regard the gift of sight far more preciously than others. Everyone who thinks seriously about the gift of sight realizes how precious it is. Nevertheless, there is no way he can have the same feelings of appreciation as a person who had been blinded.

Or take another example: a couple who was married for many years, but, G-d forbid, was not blessed with children. All couples love their children; but there is no way that the love felt by parents who have children shortly after marriage can approximate the love felt by a couple who was finally blessed with a child after many years of childlessness. Again,

---

7.   *Tanya*, ch. 7.

it is the negative experience that has made the couple more sensitive.

The same motif applies with regard to the *baal teshuvah*. His love for G-d and his commitment to the Torah and its *mitzvos* are much deeper than that of a person who did not go through a negative experience of this type.

The above explanation also sheds light on another concept we find in the Talmud. Our Sages teach[8] that a person who says, "I will sin and later I will repent," is not given the opportunity to repent.

On a simple level, this means that the person is in effect saying, "I want the best of both worlds. I want to have my cake and eat it. First, I will sin and enjoy the pleasures of this physical world. But I will not have to worry about G-d, or my reward or punishment in the World to Come. I will repent, and then I will have a clean slate. Indeed, my sins will be considered merits."

To such a person, our Sages issue a warning, "You may never be given the opportunity to repent." Since the person relies on *teshuvah,* and only because he knows that he has that option does he sin, G-d removes the opportunities for him to repent.

(It must be emphasized that if such a person strives hard, and seeks out repentance, G-d will accept his *teshuvah* as well.[9] What our Sages are saying is that in contrast to others who are helped in their path to *teshuvah,* such a person will not be granted such assistance. Indeed, he may even be hindered. Nevertheless, if he seeks to overcome these obstacles and repents with a full heart, his *teshuvah* will be accepted.)

Chassidic thought gives us a different way of understanding this passage. We are not necessarily speaking about a person who wants to sin because of his inability to control

---

8. *Yoma* 87a.
9. *Tanya, Iggeres HaTeshuvah,* Chapter 11.

his natural desires. The passage can also be referring to a very spiritual person. But this person has a difficulty. He is a *tzaddik*, a perfectly righteous man who has never sinned. And this person is envious of a *baal teshuvah*. He also wants to develop the deeper connection to G-d and more powerful love that comes forth from the *teshuvah* experience. But he does not understand how he can, for he has never sinned.[10]

And so he thinks, "Perhaps I will commit a sin." Not because he wants to sin, Heaven forbid, but so that through the cycle of sin and *teshuvah*, he will have the opportunity to develop that deeper connection to G-d.

When a person desires to sin for these reasons, his intention is good, but his thoughts are underdeveloped. It is as if a person were to say, "I will put myself in circumstances where my life will be threatened, and then the adrenaline will start flowing. I will be able to jump great distances and perform awesome feats of strength." Heaven forbid that a person should commit a sin for these reasons.

A Jew should want to do only what is right and should not invite any challenging situations, as we pray each morning,[11] "Do not lead me to sin... or to challenge." Nevertheless, our conduct is not always appropriate, and, if a person sees that he has indeed committed a sin, he should not be disheartened. On the contrary, he should realize that the sin was intended to give him the possibility of turning to G-d in *teshuvah* and developing a deeper love for Him.

And therefore, as we have said before, there is nothing that is truly negative. Everything, even those acts that are

---

10. We are speaking somewhat facetiously. In truth, every person, even a righteous man who has never sinned, has the potential to turn to G-d in *teshuvah*. For the very fact that one exists as a mortal in this material world with a sense of self implies that one's conscious processes have become separated from one's G-dly core. And thus, *teshuvah* is necessary. See the essay entitled "Teshuvah — Return, not Repentance" in *Timeless Patterns in Time* (Kehot, N.Y., 1993).
11. *Siddur Tehillat HaShem*, p. 9.

against G-d's will, can lead to good and G-dliness; it is just that they are disguised.

Therefore, when something negative happens, even if it is spiritually negative, we should not become depressed. That is a misinterpretation of the dynamic at work; one has not realized the true purpose in these events.

Take, for example, a person who is instructed by a doctor to exercise. If the person just listens to the instructions without trying to appreciate the purpose of what he is doing, he will see the exercise as a burden and a trial. Why should he work so hard?

But a person cannot remain healthy without exercise. And when a person realizes this, he does not see it as a burden. He understands that every bit of exercise he does makes him stronger and healthier. Let us take an everyday situation: In a department store there is a staircase, and right next to it, an escalator. When a person understands what exercise does for him, it is as though there is a sign there saying, "If you want to have a healthy heart, walk up the staircase." The escalator is easier; it is quicker, while the staircase requires more exertion. But climbing the stairs develops a healthy heart.

Let us take another analogy. A child comes home from school and tells his mother, "I do not want to do my homework. Please do it for me." A mother might think she should be pleasant and kind and do the homework for the child. And it would be far easier to do that than to convince the child to do his own homework.

But if the mother takes this alternative, she is handicapping her child. He will never develop his thinking processes this way. Only when the child feels a challenge and is forced to sit down and work the answers out on his own will he be able to grow intellectually. If he never expends any effort, he will grow up thinking very shallowly.

The same is true with regard to the *nisyonos*, challenges, that we face in our Divine service. They help us develop a deeper and stronger bond to G-d and His *mitzvos*.

On this basis, we can also explain another concept about which people have often wondered. Why does the soul descend to this world? Our bodies are conceived by our parents, but for a body to live, it needs a soul.

The soul existed in the spiritual realm before the person was born. Conception develops a connection between a soul and a body, but even before that connection was established the soul existed in the spiritual realm. Indeed, its existence in the spiritual realm is more vital than its subsequent corporeal existence.

In the spiritual realm, the soul only sees, hears, and experiences G-dliness. There are no physical limitations and there is no evil. Nothing negative exists there.

In the physical world, by contrast, it is impossible to appreciate G-dliness directly. And the limits of the body confine the soul's power. Moreover, we are forced to confront challenges and trials. Why is it necessary? Why can't the soul merely remain in the spiritual realm and "derive pleasure from the radiance of the Divine Presence"?[12] Why must it descend to our material earth?

To explain the purpose for this, it is useful to borrow — out of context — a concept from our Sages. Our Sages explain[13] that a descent for the purpose of an ascent is not considered a descent. Although no one can deny that a descent is taking place, since that descent has solely one purpose — the ascent that follows — it is not considered a descent, but rather a phase of the ascent.

Similarly, the descent of the soul to our material world has but one purpose: that the soul rise to a higher spiritual

---

12. *Berachos* 17a.
13. Cf. *Makkos* 7b; *Likkutei Sichos*, Vol. 29, p. 11ff.

level. Certain strengths and potentials, and a deeper level of love, do not surface when the soul is in the spiritual realm.

Why does it not surface in that realm? Because there is no challenge. It is only through the soul's descent into this physical world, where its love for G-d is threatened by all the temptations of material existence, that the soul can reach this higher peak.

Because it is being threatened, the soul strives to bring out its inner resources, and in doing so taps a deeper and more powerful source of love than could be revealed in the spiritual realms. In this way, the descent of the soul brings it to a higher rung.

The same applies with regard to the concept explained above: Even something that is spiritually negative, something that appears to be in contradiction to the observance of the Torah and its *mitzvos*, can serve a positive purpose.

When one realizes that everything that happens comes about because G-d wants it to happen, we can appreciate that it has a purpose and that purpose is good. Everything that exists and every event that transpires has G-dly energy vested within it; otherwise, it could not exist. This applies even to those experiences that appear negative; they exist because of a positive Divine purpose.

This leads to the awareness that an occurrence that appears negative is merely a test. Its negative dimension is only a disguise; what it really is, is a medium to enable one to reach a higher spiritual rung.

∽

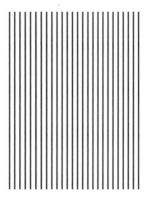

Chapter Seven
MIND-CONTROL

We have explained that a person should always be *b'simchah* because he should realize that everything that happens to him comes from G-d. Nothing is an accident, or comes about by chance. The question is, however, how to make the connection between the abstract and the actual? How can our awareness of these concepts affect our feelings?

Although a person knows that everything comes from G-d, he will often become depressed or broken when something tragic happens. What is at the core of these feelings? Is it the experience itself that causes the pain and the sorrow, or his involvement with the experience?

To clarify the question: When something happens to a person, and the person does not have the intelligence to understand that it is harmful, he will not experience pain. When do we experience pain? When we understand. And indeed, as King Solomon says:[1] "The more a person knows, the more suffering he experiences." So when a person expe-

---

1. *Ecclesiastes* 1:18.

riences pain, there are two causes for his feeling: the painful event, and his awareness of it.

When we mentioned "awareness" in the previous paragraph, we meant the person's ability to comprehend; but there is another point involved. A person can be capable of comprehending the pain of a situation, but can choose not to. If the person is tuned in to the incident that occurs, he will inevitably feel pain. But the person can choose to tune out — not pay attention to what happened. If he does this, and is successful at controlling his mind, he will not experience any pain at all.

The Modzitzer Rebbe was a great *Chassidic* leader, who composed many magnificent *Chassidic* songs. In his old age, he had to undergo an operation. Unfortunately, he had been weakened by his ailment, and the doctors were afraid to give him any anesthesia; they did not know if he would wake up. But they knew that without the operation he would not live.

They asked the Rebbe what to do, and he offered a unique suggestion: He would compose a *Chassidic* song. When the doctors would see that he is deeply engrossed in the melody, they should start the surgery.

And that is what happened. He composed the song. While they were performing the surgery, he was singing the song and he felt absolutely no pain. We have the song today. It has 36 stanzas, because the operation took quite some time.

This is not a story about a Rebbe and a miracle. Yes, he was a great Rebbe, and he performed miracles, but this particular event was natural. He was concentrating so deeply on the song, that he was not aware of anything else, and he therefore felt no pain whatsoever.

We are not *Rebbeim,* and that level of concentration is more than a little above us, but we can see parallels in our own lives. Take the following example: a person comes home from work. Something happened on the train that made him furious, and he enters the door fuming.

Suddenly, the telephone rings. It is a friend from out of town, with whom he has not spoken for months. The two friends begin talking and speak for half an hour. When the commuter hangs up, he realizes that for the past half-hour he was not upset. Why? The incident that upset him took place. The telephone call did not change that. But it did change the focus of his attention. While he was speaking, he was not thinking of what took place.

And that is why we see that certain people who endured terrible horrors — for example, people who went through the Holocaust — can nevertheless pull themselves together and rebuild their lives and their families. And there are others who have only to discover that they have lost their car keys to find themselves in the midst of a crisis.

It has to do not so much with what happens, but how much one lets what happens affect him. And this leads to another point. There are times when we hold on to memories of an unpleasant event far longer than the event calls for. We continue thinking about it day and night, morning and evening. And thinking about it so much reinforces and magnifies the pain involved.

There is an alternative. Once we stop thinking about it, the pain will cease. And this is where many of us make a basic mistake. Most people think that they are capable of controlling only their actions and their speech. They know that they can decide whether to do something or to refrain from doing it; whether to say something or not to say it. But they think that their thoughts are uncontrollable.

This is a mistake. It is true that it is harder to control thought. In contrast to speech or deed, thought is constant; there is not a moment in the day when a person is not thinking. But what to think about is subject to a person's control. He has the ability to focus his thoughts as he chooses.

If a person only realized that he has the ability to stop thinking about a certain incident, he would let go. And once he let go, he would no longer feel so much pain and sadness.

What do we mean by letting go and turning away from an undesirable thought? In the *Tanya*,[2] the Alter Rebbe says that one should push away the undesirable thought with both hands. Implicit in his words is that there are two possibilities: pushing away a thought with one hand, and pushing away a thought with two hands.

What is the difference? When an incident takes place, even when it is something that we do not want to think about, it demands our attention; naturally, our minds focus upon it and thoughts come to the fore. We have three ways of relating to these thoughts. One is to accept them, to continue to think about the subject, even though we know they are undesirable.

This approach actually encourages these thoughts to return. Think of the following analogy: A person is being bothered by someone else. Another individual is constantly ringing his doorbell and asking to be allowed into the house and to be given attention. The owner of the home really does not enjoy that person's company, but he or she does not know what to do.

There are three alternatives. The simplest is that when this person rings the doorbell, the host invites him into the house. The host sees no way out. He sits at the coffee table with his guest, offers him coffee and cake, and talks with him for two hour's time.

Although the host did not feel comfortable, his guest did. He got the attention he was looking for. And he got it in a welcome, genteel manner. He surely was not discouraged

---

2.   See Chapter 12.

from coming again. On the contrary, after being treated in this manner, it is inevitable that he will return.

There is another possibility: the host does not allow the guest into his home. He stands by the door, screaming at the person who wants to come in, and blocks his entry.

In this case, although the guest did not enter the house, he still received the host's attention. The host came to the door and talked to him. Admittedly, he did not speak to him nicely; he shouted and he screamed, but he gave the guest his attention. And so there is the possibility that the guest will return again to seek this attention, no matter how uncomfortable is the manner in which it is granted.

Then there is a third alternative: simply to ignore the person at the door entirely. In that case, he may return once, maybe twice, maybe even three times, but he will eventually stop, because there is nothing encouraging him; he is not being acknowledged at all.

The same motif will work with undesirable thoughts. If a person accepts a thought and thinks about it (even though the thought is disturbing), he has reinforced that type of thought. The attention he gives this thought pattern encourages these thoughts to proceed continually from the subconscious to the conscious, even though they cause him discomfort.

One may try to stop the thoughts, to prevent them from coming to mind. But often this means that the person is fighting himself and repeatedly telling himself not to think about these particular thoughts. But like the host shouting at the guest at the door, he is giving these thoughts attention. That is what we mean by pushing away a thought with one hand. With one hand you are pushing the thought away, but since you are paying attention to it, you are bringing it closer to yourself with the other hand.

In other words, when I am thinking that I should not be thinking about a particular subject, I am still paying attention to thoughts that I do not want to encourage. I am acknowledging these thoughts, and in so doing, I am inviting the thoughts to proceed from the subconscious to the conscious.

There is another alternative. When a thought comes to the person's mind, he can refuse to pay any attention to it. He need not make the effort to push it out of his mind. He can simply ignore it, and focus his attention on a different subject altogether. And when he ignores a thought and does not acknowledge it at all, this thought pattern eventually will no longer seek his attention.

Most people will ask: "How can I think about anything else? This thought keeps coming to my mind."

A person once came to the Maggid of Mezeritch with this problem. "My mind is always straying. How can I control my thoughts?"

"See my disciple, R. Zev of Zhitomer. He will help you," the Maggid answered.

And so, the person journeyed to see R. Zev. He arrived in Zhitomer at night, and only with difficulty was he able to locate R. Zev's house. Finally he reached the *tzaddik's* home and banged loudly on the door, anxious to be invited in from the cold.

There was no answer. He banged again, and still no answer. Upset, he continued to bang with all his might, but no one inside responded. Annoyed, but with no other alternative, he was forced to spend the night outside.

In the morning, R. Zev welcomed him warmly. The visitor told the *tzaddik* why he had come and R. Zev invited him to partake of his hospitality for as long as he desired. He was more than slightly curious at the difference between this reception and the cold shoulder he had been given the previous night, but in deference to the *tzaddik,* he remained silent.

He stayed at R. Zev's home for several days, sharing talks with the *tzaddik* and learning from observing his everyday conduct. But one thing bothered him. He had come with a specific intent, to learn how to control his thoughts, and R. Zev had not given him any instruction with regard to this matter.

Finally, he broached the question to the *tzaddik*. "The Maggid sent me here for a reason," he told his host. "Why haven't you taught me how to control my thoughts?"

"But I already have," answered R. Zev.

"When?"

"The first night you came, you banged and banged on the door to my home, trying to come in. I knew you were there, but decided not to let you enter. And I kept to that decision no matter how hard you banged. That's the secret of controlling your thoughts."

It's true, this is not easy. But a person has an alternative. No one can think about two things at the same time. And so, when a person forces himself to start thinking about another subject, the undesired thoughts will fade away.

True, they may come back ten minutes later, but once again the person has the alternative of controlling his thoughts and thinking of something else. The undesired thoughts may return again twenty minutes later, but again, the person can think about another subject.

Eventually, if he keeps ignoring the undesirable thought long enough, it will cease surfacing from the subconscious to the conscious. At first, it will surface less often than before. Ultimately, it will stop surfacing entirely.

To explain by analogy: Our muscles are strengthened by exercise. If we do not exercise a muscle, the muscle becomes weaker. If a person is, G-d forbid, bedridden for several months because of a back problem, he may have trouble walking when he is finally able to get out of bed. His ailment may not have affected the muscles of his feet, but the inactivity did.

We have many thoughts and experiences in our subconscious minds. When we allow them to come up to the conscious level, it is like exercising a muscle. This means that in addition to the fact that we are focusing on these thoughts now, we are also encouraging these thoughts to emerge continually from the subconscious.[3]

When, however, a person does not allow a thought to surface, and pushes it away with two hands — i.e., he ignores it entirely — he diminishes the probability of its surfacing in the future. It is possible that the thought will recur again, and perhaps recur several times. But each time it is ignored, its tendency to recur will be weakened.

When, by contrast, a person pushes away a thought with one hand — i.e., he acknowledges the thought and thinks how not to think about it — he is, in fact, inviting this thought; it is like a form of exercise. He allows the thought to capture his attention, and this encourages the thought to continue surfacing from the subconscious to the conscious.

A man and a woman once came to a rabbi, and the woman demanded a divorce. The problem was that her husband would come home drunk and would say all sorts of unpleasant things to his wife. In response, she would scream at him. He would then throw something at her; she would throw something else back at him. And World War III would break loose — almost every night.

Despite the difficulties, the rabbi saw that the marriage had potential, even a lot of potential, if both people would only learn to modify their conduct. So he asked the woman

---

3. Although we are talking about undesirable thoughts, thoughts that we would like to prevent from surfacing, the same pattern applies regarding desirable thoughts. When a person continually thinks about positive things, such thoughts will also arise on their own accord.

to give it one more try, and he promised that if this did not work, he would make sure that the divorce went through.

What did the rabbi suggest? He told the woman, "I have an ancient book of *Kabbalah* that contains a remedy for strife between a husband and his wife." He continued to give the woman detailed instructions: She was to take a bottle that holds exactly eight ounces to a *mikveh* after midnight on *Rosh Chodesh*, the first day of the month. She should fill the bottle with water three times, and pour out the water three times. Afterwards, she should fill the bottle again, wrap it in a bag so that others would not see it, and take it home.

"When your husband comes home," the rabbi continued, "take a teaspoon of this water. Do not spit it out, and do not swallow it until your husband is asleep."

After much effort, the woman prepared the bottle and the water. That night, she heard her husband coming home. From the distance, she heard that he was drunk and that he was saying very unpleasant things.

Obediently, she took the water, put a teaspoon in her mouth, and held it there. Her husband walked into the house and started to shout and scream, insulting her. Of course, she was dying to scream back at him, but she could not — she had the water in her mouth. And so, her husband continued to scream and shout for half an hour.

Finally, because he got no feedback, he grew tired and fell asleep. After he fell asleep, the woman hurried to spit out the water. She began to scream and shout and release all the antagonism that had been building up when he was letting loose. But it did not bother her husband. He was snoring away; he did not hear anything she said.

The following day, the same thing happened. He came home and started screaming and shouting, but she could not answer him, because she had the water in her mouth. But this day, there was a change — he screamed and shouted for only 25 minutes, and then he fell asleep.

Day after day, the scene repeated itself, but each time the husband shouted a little bit less. Soon he shouted for only a minute or two, and after a while, he stopped shouting altogether.

When the shouting stopped, they were able to communicate with each other. Once they could talk to each other, they were eventually able to start appreciating each other.

Was the remedy the rabbi suggested written in the *Kabbalah?* Well, not explicitly, but the *Kabbalah* does teach the virtues of forbearance. What the rabbi was saying was in essence, "Ignore him, and let him reach equilibrium. And then you will see that things will be able to be worked out." And it was successful. Why? Because by ignoring something, you discourage it entirely.

The same concept applies with regard to our thoughts. The key is pushing away an undesirable thought with both hands, turning our minds to another point of focus and letting the undesired thought flow out of our consciousness naturally, without effort.

Chassidus highlights the power of our minds, and teaches us that the mind is the key to the emotions.[4] Just like a key with which one can either turn the engine of a car on or off, by focusing or turning off our mental attention, we can control our emotions.

To change events that have happened is not within our power; they are history. But we can change the nature of how we will react to whatever has happened. We have full control over our minds, and can decide what we want to think about and what we do not want to think about. And when we employ such control, we then become masters of our emotions.

Take, for example, feelings of anger. As we mentioned earlier, our Sages teach that a person who becomes angry

---

4.   *Derech Mitzvoṣecha* p. 46.

and loses his temper is considered as if he worshipped idols. One might ask: if a person is provoked and becomes angry, is it not better that he let loose? Modern psychology says that if a person allows pressure to build up inside of him, it can cause problems. The person becomes like a pressure cooker, and this can even affect his health. If, however, he lets his temper loose, it will relieve the pressure and he will be able to relax and be himself again. Why then does the Torah tell us not to release the anger?

There are two resolutions to this question: First, one can sublimate the anger and express its energy in a positive form. The way a person expresses himself does not have to be destructive. The same energy can be released through positive channels. Instead of letting loose with anger, a person can grit his teeth and apply himself with determination to a challenge he faces.

Moreover, if the energy is burning within a person, it may be better for him to let it out. What the Torah demands of a person, however, is not to reach that point — never to let his blood become boiling inside.

Why does a person become full of anger? Not because of what has happened, but because he is *thinking* about what happened, and concentrating on it. We have an alternative. There is no need to feed these fires. We can divert our thoughts from the disturbing factor and concentrate on something else.

The challenge is not to work on methods of letting out the pressure, but to be a step ahead; to work on a way to prevent the pressure from building up in the first place. And this means disciplining our thoughts.

This is a basic principle of Torah. Just as a person should discipline his actions and his speech, a person must discipline his thoughts. When a person makes the effort to discipline his thoughts, eventually he will attain control.

Take jealousy, for example. If a person sees something that another person has, and his natural reaction is to become jealous, he may not be able to change this natural response easily. What he can do is not occupy himself with thoughts of jealousy. There he has control.

He may not be able to help a jealous thought from surfacing from the subconscious to the conscious. That is a natural response. But to continue to pursue such thoughts and to dwell upon them, there a person can — and must — exercise control.

Whenever a jealous thought comes to mind, one should stop and divert his attention. The thought may still return several times. Nevertheless, eventually, as one continues to exercise control, these thoughts of jealousy will become far less frequent. Ultimately, they will cease surfacing from the subconscious to the conscious.

And the same concept applies with regard to thoughts of hatred. The Torah tells us not to hate another Jew.[5] But what happens if another person hurts us terribly? It is only natural for feelings of hatred to be aroused. How can we control them?

The answer is that it is indeed very difficult to change our insides so that we do not react with anger or hatred in such an instance. That may be beyond our control. Once such a thing takes place, thoughts of hatred will probably begin to surface.

But here is where we should exercise control. We have the ability to stop ourselves from occupying our minds with thoughts of hatred.

How can we stop ourselves? Not by pushing the hatred away with one hand, but by totally cutting it off, by switching to a different topic entirely. This prevents the feelings of

---

5.   *Leviticus* 19:17.

hatred from being reinforced and magnified. They will not flare up, but eventually will subside.

These thoughts of hatred may continue coming back. Nevertheless, when they are ignored once, a second time, a third time and even a hundredth time, they will eventually stop surfacing from the subconscious to the conscious.

Many of us can look back in our past and find that when we were younger, we were obsessed with certain things. We wanted them and could not stop thinking about them. In the morning, in the afternoon, during school, during meals, at night, when we fell asleep, in our dreams; it was almost as if this were all we thought about.

When we think back now, we ask ourselves, "What happened? Why am I no longer obsessed with these same thoughts? What changed?" Often the situation did not change and we never had this desire satisfied.

Why then do we not continue to think about it? The answer is very simple. Several years have passed, and in the interim we have been confronted with new situations, new desires and new problems, and maybe even new obsessions. We have devoted so much time and attention to these new matters, that we lost interest in the old ones. We paid less and less attention to them, and eventually we stopped thinking about them altogether.

This is what we should do with feelings of depression and all negative thoughts. In general, we should know that everything that happens is good and, therefore, a person should always be b'simchah, filled with real joy. We should internalize this idea and make it part of us. This will help us not lose our equilibrium when undesirable things happen.

But if something is able to cause us to become upset, we should know that we have an alternative. That alternative does not involve meditating on how the upsetting factor is, in reality, good which is disguised. A person who is very upset will not always honestly be able to come to such a realization. What we can do — and what we must do, if we want to preserve our inner balance — is to turn our attention to another subject — and do so again and again until we are no longer bothered by the upsetting thought. Once we are not being controlled by our depressing thoughts, we can focus on the truth that Torah teaches: that everything comes from G-d and is in essence good.

∞

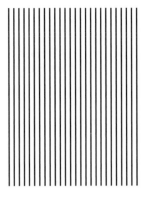

Chapter Eight
GROWING FROM PAIN

In the previous chapter, we explained that even if an event takes place that could plunge a person into depression and sadness, he can remain *b'simchah,* full of joy. Instead of allowing these negative qualities to dominate him, he has the potential to discipline his thoughts and divert his attention to another subject. Because he is not thinking about an incident, he will not experience pain or depression. He will be able to build the inner resources that enable him to overcome this challenge.

The question, however, remains: Is it not important that a person experience pain when things are not working out, for this will spur him to improve? If a person never experiences pain because he constantly distracts the mind with other subjects or avoids the issue entirely, the problem — be it something physical or something spiritual — will never be dealt with.

On a physical level, physicians say that pain can be a blessing, because when a person experiences pain, it makes him aware of a problem. It motivates him to go to a physician, undergo an examination, and enable the problem to be discovered. Then, as the old *Chassidic* adage says, "the knowledge of the disease is half the cure." When a problem is defined, it can be eliminated.

If, G-d forbid, a person never experiences any pain, the disease or malfunction will continue to grow. It is possible that by the time it is discovered, it would be too late to do anything about it. Therefore, the fact that pain brings the condition to the person's attention and thus enables him to deal with it, is obviously a positive quality.

Why, then, should we avoid emotional pain? Why not say that when a person feels pain about a certain event, it is positive — that the pain is a force pushing him to change? There is tremendous inertia when it comes to changing our personalities, and without such motivation it is questionable whether a person would in fact change.

A *farbrengen* is a gathering where *chassidim* sit together and sing *Chassidic* songs. Usually, an elder *chassid* speaks to his younger colleagues and encourages them to improve their Divine service. Once, a group of *chassidim* were sitting together in a dark basement, wrapped up in such a gathering. Another person was walking by and heard singing. Recognizing the melody, he called out, "Where are you? Where is the *farbrengen*?"

One of the *chassidim* called back to him and told him to come down to the basement. After taking several steps down the staircase, he hesitated because it was very dark. He called down again, "How can I go down there? It is dark. I cannot see where I am going."

One of the *chassidim* sitting by the table answered him, "Do not worry, if you sit here long enough, your eyes will get used to the darkness."

The *chassid* was telling him a simple physiological fact. When we sit in darkness for a time, our pupils expand and we can see better than we could when we first entered the room. But the elder *chassid* conducting the *farbrengen* wanted to focus on a different dimension. "That is precisely the problem," he told his listeners. "If you sit in darkness long enough, you get used to it. You do not realize the need for light."

This is why it can be positive for a person to feel pain in a given situation. If something hurts him, he will know that something is wrong, and this will push him to change. If, instead, he is allowed to remain complacent, he will make his peace with the problem without trying to solve it.

Whenever a person has problems — be they physical, financial, or spiritual — it is very important for him to recognize that there is a difficulty and to do something about correcting it. Why should we tell him to divert his attention and ignore the matter? Of what permanent value is such bliss?

On the other hand, sadness and depression are not always valuable. On the contrary, they are often paralyzing influences that rob a person of vitality and prevent him from solving the problems that present themselves.

Thus, it appears that there are two types of feeling bad: one that stirs positive change, and one that reinforces negativity. How can we recognize the difference between the two? In truth, when a person is experiencing feelings of remorse, regret or hurt, he may not be able to recognize which of the two types of feeling he is experiencing. Afterwards, however, he can tell by the results.

Let us take an example: A person is up late at night and thinks to himself, "There are so many things that I wanted to get done this past month. But I did not do them. This was not done, and that was not done." The person continues along this train of thought until he comes to the conclusion, "I am a failure."

All the pressure from the entire month piles up on him, and he feels miserable and depressed. And what does he do?

He decides he cannot face the world anymore. So he dives into bed, covers himself with his blankets and goes to sleep.

Perhaps this is a slight exaggeration. The point is, however, that feeling bad can leave one drained of energy with no incentive to do anything except escape from the world.

The same situation — a person sitting up at night and realizing that he has failed to accomplish anything in a month — can produce a totally different response. Instead of wanting to go to sleep, the person can feel charged with energy and filled with the resolve that he will get the job done.

What prompted these feelings? His feeling bad about his lack of accomplishment. In this instance, feeling bad generated energy and vitality.

In the *Tanya*,[1] the Alter Rebbe differentiates between these two types of feeling bad. The depression that dulls a person's sensitivity and should be avoided is termed *atzvus*. The type of feeling bad that spurs a person towards positive activity is referred to as *merirus*, "bitterness."

To differentiate between the two, a person has to ask himself: "Why am I feeling bad? Is it concern with the past or with the future?" If the person is upset about something that has happened, and all he can think about is how bad it was, then it is *atzvus*. There is absolutely no purpose in concentrating on such thoughts; the event is over. There is nothing to do about it. What the person should do is get all thoughts of it out of his system entirely.

If, however, when thinking about a problem a person is prompted to do something about it, then it is *merirus*; it is the kind of feeling bad that is valuable. True, the person feels regret and remorse, but his feelings are channeled in the direction of change. He keeps asking himself: "What can I do

---

1.   Chapter 31.

to correct the situation?" and "How can I see that it does not happen again?"

There is, however, a problem. Man is not a robot, and it is hard to discern the fine line that differentiates between these positive thoughts of regret and remorse and the undesirable thoughts of depression. How can we make sure that our negative thoughts remain directed to a positive purpose?

The answer again centers on mind control. We should regulate the amount of time we spend thinking about these things. This enables us to exercise control over our thoughts, instead of allowing these thoughts to control us. Bitterness is a positive quality, but only in small doses, and only at an appropriate time.

It can be compared to an antibiotic. An antibiotic is often a helpful drug that cures disease. But people take antibiotics in very small dosages, usually a teaspoon two or three times a day.

If you are drinking apple juice or orange juice, you may drink an entire cup or even two cups. And you may drink as often as you want. But we do not take antibiotics in such large quantities, and we do not take them very often.

Why not? Because antibiotics are fundamentally a destructive agent. It is true that they destroy the germs that are causing illness. But they can — and if they are taken too frequently, they will — destroy life systems within the body that are necessary for our health.

Therefore, they are taken only in small amounts. This enables the destructive activity to be controlled and to be directed to purging the bacteria-causing illness without affecting the well-being of the body as a whole.

Similar concepts apply with regard to remorse and regret. Feeling remorse and regret is itself a negative quality. Sometimes, however, it is effective in rectifying an undesirable situation. Nevertheless, because it is fundamentally destructive, it has to be regulated and employed within certain limits. Only then will it be controlled and directed toward a positive intent. Otherwise, it will lead to depression and will drain a person's energy.

To cite an analogy: There are activities that are very good and are considered to be great *mitzvos*. Nevertheless, if these same activities are performed at the wrong time or in the wrong place, they can lose all positive value, and even become negative. For example, eating *matzah* is a very great *mitzvah*. But when? When we eat the *matzah* on the night of Passover, at the *seder*. If we eat *matzah* at any other time, it is not a *mitzvah*. And if we eat the *matzah* on the night of Yom Kippur, it is considered a sin, a very severe violation of Torah law.

The same thing is true about fasting. It is also a very great *mitzvah*. But when? On Yom Kippur, the holiest day of the year. At other times, it is not as important. And if we fast on the night of Passover, when we are supposed to be eating *matzah,* we have done something wrong.

The same idea applies with regard to thinking about problems — whether spiritual or material — that a person must correct. There is positive value to such thought and it should be encouraged. But only at the right time and in the right way. Otherwise, not only are such thoughts not positive, they can become destructive.

How can such thoughts become negative? Here we can learn an interesting concept from the Hebrew language. The Hebrew word for "sadness" is *atzvus* (עצבות). The Hebrew word for laziness is *atzlus* (עצלות). They are spelled in a very similar way. The only difference is that one contains a *beis* (ב) and the other, a *lamed* (ל).

What is the connection between depression and laziness? The connection works both ways. Depression leads to laziness. When a person is depressed, he is drained of energy. And this inactivity reinforces itself; the person becomes lazy.

The converse, however, is also true. Laziness leads to depression. A person allows himself to get depressed because it is an easier alternative. Otherwise, he would have to come to terms with the problem, to face himself and work out a solution. But that requires effort; and there is less work in lying back and feeling depressed.

Many times when a person is depressed, a friend will knock on his door and say, "Come on. We are going someplace. Do you want to join us?" And the person will refuse to go with them. The person knows that if he went along with his friend, he would definitely be able to pull himself out of his depression. He would start thinking about what is happening now, and that would take his mind off what is causing his depression. But he just cannot let go.

Why can he not let go? Because by staying depressed, he need not face the challenge of living.

When a person faces himself and confronts the problems he must deal with, it is not difficult to arrive at a solution. Many people say that they spend a lot of time thinking about a problem, but they can never arrive at a solution. Why is that so? Because at the outset, their thoughts were not directed toward finding a solution.

On the contrary, what they wanted to do — although they might not be aware of it — is to continue thinking about how devastating the situation is, and how if such and such would happen, it would be even worse.

There are times when we enjoy focusing on negativity. It is illogical. We know that these thoughts are not really relevant, that they will not bring us genuine satisfaction, nor will they lead to a practical solution. And yet we continue to think about them. Why? Because we are not ready to go out and face life. We would rather wallow in the dumps of despair instead of going out and trying to solve the problem.

If a person eliminated all that negativity and focused on one thing — how he can solve the problem he is confronting — he would be surprised to find that within a short period of time, he will conceive of several possible solutions to any given problem.

One of the *mashpi'im* (spiritual mentors) in the Lubavitcher *yeshivah* in Russia in the 1920's was R. Yechezkel Feigen. He would teach *Chassidic* thought, and from time to time, he would gather his students together and lead a *farbrengen* for them.

At one such *farbrengen*, he demanded a lot of his students. He told them that he wanted to see a deeper commitment to prayer, to study, and to personal development. His words were touched with intensity, and he addressed his students personally, showing them where they needed to concentrate their efforts.

They were deeply moved by what he said and many began to cry. Suddenly in the midst of the *farbrengen*, the person appointed as watchman came running with the news that the KGB was carrying out a search in the area.

This represented a real danger. Needless to say, such a gathering was prohibited; all of the participants could have been sent to hard-labor camps. Immediately, everyone began suggesting alternatives. One said, "Let us try to flee." Another suggested turning off the light, hoping darkness would serve as a cover. A third thought about putting newspapers and political science books on the table to show that they were involved in activities that the government would accept.

Thank G-d, the KGB never came to the room. They left the area as abruptly as they came, and the rabbi and the students were able to sit down to resume the *farbrengen*. The rabbi turned to his students and told them, "I just saw something very strange. I hope you can explain it to me."

The students looked at him quizzically and he continued, "Tell me, what affects you more, a difficulty in spiritual matters or a problem involving material things?"

The students were honest with themselves, and with him. Immediately, they replied that it was material things that affected them more.

"Why then," he asked, "was it that when I spoke to you about your spiritual well-being, everybody was crying, but when you heard that the KGB was in the area and your lives were in danger, nobody cried?"

One of the students gave him a puzzled look and replied, "What did you expect us to do, sit down and cry? What good would that do? We had to figure out a way either to get out or to hide ourselves before they came."

R. Feigen had been waiting for such an answer. "Oh, I see. When you had to act fast, you knew that crying would not help. Why, then, when it comes to spiritual things is it acceptable to cry?"

He repeated this concept and explained it until it sank in. The students understood that crying can be merely an excuse. It does not solve the problem at all. All it does is give the person catharsis. When, by contrast, a person is serious about making a change, he does not have time to cry. Every moment is precious and can be used to implement a solution. That is the way it is supposed to be.

In summary, what we are saying is that *Chassidus* teaches us that there are two ways of responding to negative factors — whether they be physical or spiritual. One is positive, *merirus*, which is translated as bitterness, and the other is negative, *atzvus*, which we have translated as depression.

There are four fundamental differences between the two: a) *Atzvus* has no life to it; it is the type of feeling bad that leaves one drained. The person loses his incentive to do anything. *Merirus,* by contrast, spurs energy; it has dynamism and life.

b) *Atzvus* perpetuates itself. The feelings of depression continue for a long time. With *merirus,* feeling bad is temporary. The positive drive it brings produces active feelings of achievement in a very short time.

c) *Atzvus* is not directed toward a practical solution. It is not a means to an end; it is an end in itself. One becomes satisfied thinking about how terrible everything is. *Merirus,* by contrast, is future-oriented and focuses on a solution and the future. The person asks himself: what can I do about the problem?

d) *Atzvus* leads a person to be more withdrawn and self-concerned. He thinks more and more about himself. The dynamism of *merirus,* by contrast, allows a person to think about others.

There are many ramifications of the difference between these two approaches. For example, a suggestion was once made to remember the six million Jews who died in the Holocaust by leaving an empty chair at the *seder* table Pesach night. Seeing that there is something missing at our *seder* table would cause us to remember the six million.

The Lubavitcher Rebbe disagreed with this suggestion for two reasons. Firstly, Pesach is a holiday; a time when we are not allowed to do anything that is associated with mourning and sadness. Even if he had appreciated the idea, the timing was inappropriate.

Secondly, the Rebbe emphasized that the suggestion put the focus on the negative. The Rebbe agreed that there should be an extra chair at the *seder.* But why, he asked, should it be empty? Let it be filled by a person who, had he not received this invitation, would not have attended a *seder* at all.

The Rebbe was not just offering a different suggestion. He was showing an entirely different approach to the issue. Instead of having our thinking about the loss of six million Jews result in an empty chair, he wanted that the emotion aroused be directed to a positive purpose.

What can be done to compensate for the loss of the six million? First and foremost, something positive. Take a Jew who is alive today and is on the way to total assimilation — he doesn't even seek to take part in a Pesach *Seder* — and make him feel part of the Jewish people. This counteracts Hitler's efforts and demonstrates that nothing — neither Pharaoh, nor Hitler, nor for that matter the openness of American society — can break the connection that a Jew shares with his spiritual heritage.

Let us take another example. One of the main concerns of many people who have changed their way of life and begun to observe the Torah and its *mitzvos* is *kashrus*. Once people begin keeping kosher and learn how important it is, many become quite upset about having eaten non-*kosher* food for so many years.

I know a number of people who wrote letters to the Lubavitcher Rebbe asking his advice regarding what they should do to atone for all the non-*kosher* food that they had eaten. They expected the Rebbe to tell them to fast a few times a week, to refrain from eating foods that gave them pleasure or to offer other suggestions of that type. The Rebbe, however, took a totally different approach. He told them to encourage and to educate other Jews to observe the laws of *kashrus*.

What the Rebbe was saying was: do not focus on the pain you are feeling because of your errors. Transform that pain into positive and productive energy. Reach out to another person and share your insights with him.

For *merirus* to be an effective tool in spurring us to improve our conduct, it cannot be left to spontaneity.

Personal growth depends on a person's controlling his feelings, and that control does not happen spontaneously.

For this reason, there has to be a designated time when we think about the different problems that we have. Whether the problems are physical, financial or family oriented, we cannot allow them to haunt us all day long. Nor can we forfeit control when we think about them. We have to set aside a time when we are prepared to confront them.

Even spiritual failings should only be dealt with at a time set aside explicitly for that purpose. *Chassidus* talks about setting aside time to think about our spiritual well-being. It calls such thoughts *cheshbon hanefesh*, which literally means "making an account for the soul."

Various times are designated for this: daily — at the end of the day before going to bed; weekly — towards the end of the week, on Thursday night; monthly — on the last day of the month, which is known as *Yom Kippur Katan*, "a miniature Yom Kippur"; and yearly — at the end of the year, throughout the month of Elul.

These practices emphasize that, as mentioned above, there has to be a designated time to think about these matters. We cannot let these thoughts just barge in on us at any given time. We also see that the designated time is always at the end of the period in question.

During the day, a person should be active and productive, focusing on accomplishment. It is not a time to sit back and review situations; it is a time to act. When the day is coming to an end and he is preparing for the next day, he should stop and ask himself, "How did the day pass?" and "What can I do so that tomorrow will be better than today?"

The same concept applies to a weekly cycle, a monthly cycle and a yearly cycle. At the end, we should take stock of what we are doing, so that we are prepared for the new cycle that is approaching. But before the end of that cycle, we should be busy working, doing productive things that will benefit both ourselves and others.[2]

On this basis, we can explain the conclusion reached in the previous chapter. A person should dismiss negative thoughts from his mind, that is true — but only when he is feeling depression, not bitterness. Even if he is feeling bitterness, but it is at the wrong time, such as when he is supposed to be at work, *davening*, studying or busy with the family, these thoughts should be dismissed.

At all times, we should be in control. We should bring the undesirable matter to our attention when we want to, and deal with it in the way we know best. This is a productive approach.

---

2.   See *Likkutei Sichos*, Vol. 16, p. 272.

itself, but the fact that we are thinking about it. If a person were able to dismiss from his mind the thoughts that upset him, he would not experience so much discomfort.

This concept also requires an explanation. If it is so much more comfortable just to dismiss negative thoughts from our minds, why do we not do it easily? Why do we find that one of the most difficult things for people to do is to dismiss these negative thoughts from their minds? Why is it so difficult to let go? Why do we hold on to something that is destructive?

There is one point lying at the core of both issues: *yeshus*. *Yeshus* means obsession with *self*. It is important for a person to have a positive self-image. A person should feel strong, confident, and resilient. Without such positive feelings, he will not function successfully in his relations with others — nor for that matter, in his relations with G-d.[1]

But *yeshus* is more than a positive self-image; it is an approach in which *self* lies at the core of the person's being and dominates — consciously and subconsciously — the person's approach to life. This approach is the source of depression. Everything that happens to such a person, whatever goes on in his life, revolves around one question: how does it affect his *self*?

Things are bound to happen to every person that do not fit his ideal of the way things should be. And it is likely that all of us from time to time will fail in certain objectives, or be hurt by other people. When a person is involved with his ego, these factors will hurt his sense of self and make him feel bad. But what is worse is that he holds tight to the hurt and does not let go. He cannot let go, because it is his *self* that is involved, and his *self* is all that he is concerned with.

A person who is not focused on himself can let go. We do not always succeed. Our dreams are not always fulfilled, and not all our relationships work out. A person who is not

---

1. *Maamar VaYasufu Anavim (Sefer HaMaamarim 5710, p. 237ff).*

very self-concerned can, however, look past a temporary failure, go on with his life, and do so with happiness.

There are no absolutes here. Everybody thinks about himself, but the question is: "in which way?" Take the following example: A physician treats a patient who has a difficult disease, and he succeeds in curing him. He will surely be happy, but there are two possible reasons for his happiness.

The first focuses on the good he has accomplished. A person was suffering, his life was in danger, and now the person will be able to live a happy and fruitful life and continue to bring joy to his family.

The second reason focuses on the physician's own power of achievement. He is proud and happy that he was the one able to effect the cure. It is his feelings of *self* that bring him happiness.

The same holds true when, G-d forbid, the situation is reversed — when the physician works very hard to save a patient's life, but realizes that he may not be successful. One type of person will be very upset because a person is dying. He sees the sad faces of everybody in the family, and that hurts him and causes him pain.

The other type of person will also be upset, but his main thought will be "I failed." He will be upset that he was not able to cure the patient — not so much for the patient's sake, but more for his own. He is hurt when he does not succeed.

We all are motivated by both these thrusts. Each of us shares a certain degree of sensitivity to others, and every one of us has a certain measure of self-concern. The question is, however, what is the person's prime motivating factor.

A *yesh*, a person preoccupied with himself, is motivated by his ego. This is what pushes him forward throughout the day. In contrast, a person who is *buttel*, selfless, is focused on the goals he seeks to accomplish. He is also conscious of his *self*. He takes responsibility and knows that others are relying on him. But his *self* — whether he succeeds or fails — is not his main point of focus. His attention is centered on goals and objectives.

Take the following example: A person gets up in front of a crowd of 500 people to deliver a lecture. In such a situation, he is very conscious of himself and what he is doing. Let us take the same person in a totally different situation: he gets on a bus and drops a token into the register. Does he know he is walking onto the bus? Yes. Does he know that he is dropping the token in? Yes. Is he thinking of himself in the same way he thinks of himself when he is standing on stage before all those people? Absolutely not.

When we carry out our ordinary day-to-day activities, we are aware of what we are doing, but we do not attach any self-importance to the deed. Our approach is matter-of-fact, to deal with the situation in front of us. But when we are on stage, or in other situations where we are singled out for attention, we become conscious of our *selves*; we think of how we appear to others and what they think of us.

We see from this that there are two ways of functioning. One way is to focus on what I am doing; the task in front of me. And the other is to focus on the fact that I am doing it, to see myself more than the task I have to perform.

A *yesh* is a person who puts the focus on himself. His thoughts revolve around himself, and how everything he encounters will affect him.

Bittul, the opposite of *yeshus*, means nullifying the *self*. But it does not mean crushing one's personality; it means dedicating oneself to a higher purpose than *self*, and constantly striving to achieve that purpose. When a person is *buttel*, he functions without being aware of himself. And that is healthy and natural. On the contrary, it is unnatural for a person to be self-conscious.

A professor of podiatry was teaching his students about the movement of the feet. He explained how the various nerves, muscles, sinews, and bones in the foot combine to work in harmony to enable us to walk. After he finished his lecture, he walked out of the classroom and headed through the campus toward his home. He began thinking of the dynamics of his movement, how moving his foot requires the synchronized function of so many different parts of the body. And he tried to sense how these different functions were taking place as he proceeded.

Can you imagine what happened? The more he thought, the clumsier his gait became, and soon he could not walk at all. His feet would not move.

How was he able to start walking again? By dismissing the entire subject from his mind. He started thinking about a different idea and paid no attention to his feet; only then was he able to walk. For when a person becomes too involved with the fact that he is doing something, he loses his ability to function naturally.

There is another similar story: A rabbi was once walking down the street. A passerby stopped him and admired his long white beard. The rabbi smiled graciously. The passerby then asked a question: "Rabbi, when you sleep at night, is your beard underneath your blanket or on top of your blanket?"

The rabbi looked very puzzled and said, "To tell you the truth, I have absolutely no idea."

The passerby did not understand. "You have had this beard for over forty years. Don't you know what happens with it at night?"

The rabbi told him, "I simply do not know."

For the next two weeks, the rabbi could not fall asleep. First, he put his beard under his blanket and he felt uncomfortable. Then he put it on top of the blanket and he felt uncomfortable. He could not find a comfortable position.

How did he sleep for forty years? When he did not think about the question, he never had a problem. When did his problems begin? When he started thinking consciously about something that should come naturally.

And that is true about so many other things. When we are busy living our lives and accomplishing things, we do not think about all the things we are doing. When our minds are focused on what has to be done, we function happily and successfully. But when a person becomes self-absorbed and starts thinking about how everything affects him — that is not the natural way and it causes problems.

The differences between *yeshus* and *bittul* also lie at the heart of the differences between *atzvus* and *merirus* mentioned before. We asked: why does a person find it so difficult to let go? If he is a *yesh*, he cannot do that because his entire life revolves around his sense of self. He might understand that it is better to let go, but he cannot. Although it brings him only irritation and discomfort, he will continue moping about a given situation and chewing over the particulars, time and time again. It is as if he has no other alternative. He is too tied to his *self*; that is what his life is all about.

But a person who is tuned into the deeper dimension of his being, the G-dliness that is within him, is not attached to his *self* to so great a degree. If something unpleasant happens, he is prepared to let go. He has other things on his mind; he is thinking about the other tasks he wants to accomplish and is looking toward the future, not to the past. Moreover, a person who is characterized by *bittul* is more accepting of G-d and His plan. In contrast, when a person is a *yesh*, his self-preoccupation interferes with the acceptance of G-d's will, for his ego cannot bear giving up control.

Another difference between *merirus* and *atzvus* is that a person who experiences *atzvus* does not think in terms of a practical solution. He just thinks in terms of how bad it is and how much worse it can get, what this one thinks about him, and how he is really not that bad; after all, compare him to his brother, his sister, his cousin or his next-door neighbor. These are the sort of thoughts that go through the mind of a depressed person. And in a certain way, these thoughts grant him a form of satisfaction.

A person who tastes *merirus,* by contrast, is motivated to seek a solution to the problem. He is not self-absorbed; he has committed himself to goals and purposes, and he looks at what happens in his life and in his environment in terms of these purposes. He is prepared to confront the problems that he faces, his own faults, and even his own mistakes. At the time he tastes *merirus,* he feels pain — real pain, the kind of pain that comes from an honest appreciation of a situation that requires improvement, not the self-made pain that comes from ego obsession; but this is only a temporary feeling. Overall, he is happy, with the true sense of happiness that comes from being dedicated to a purpose and nurturing it to fulfillment.

The bottom line is that what causes depression is *yeshus,* a person's obsession with his own ego that prevents him from focusing on his purpose in life and the intent G-d designated for him. Such a person will remain obsessed with himself and will be unable to experience the true joy that comes from totally accepting G-d and His plan and becoming an active partner in its expression.

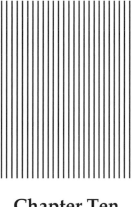

Chapter Ten
LETTING GO

A story[1] is told about a king who was once seriously ill. All the physicians despaired of curing him. One healer offered a remedy: If the king would put on the shirt of a person who is absolutely happy, then the king would be healed.

Immediately, riders were dispatched all over the country to look for a person who is absolutely happy and bring his shirt back to the king. First they went to the richest person in the country. They asked him, "Are you happy?"

He answered: "Of course. I am the richest person in the country."

"But are you absolutely happy?"

He began to hesitate. "Absolute is a difficult term. How can I be absolutely happy? I always have to protect my position. Take, for example, the businessman in the north. His concerns have been thriving and I am worried about the

---

1.   See *Sefer HaMaamarim 5710*, p. 237ff.

possibility of competition. And I've had a setback or two recently . . . ."

The messengers left him in the middle of his thoughts. They saw that despite his wealth he was worried, and he did not know what true happiness was.

Then they ran to the person who was the country's leading educational figure. "Are you happy?" they asked him. "Yes," he answered. "Absolutely happy?" And there he began to hem and haw. He told them about his unfulfilled desires and how he feels threatened by certain people. And they saw that he also did not know what absolute happiness meant.

And they went from person to person and it was always the same story. Some people were outwardly happy, and some were inwardly happy. But no one was absolutely happy. Beneath the surface, everyone was burdened by various worries, concerns and anxieties.

After this long and unsuccessful journey, they decided it was time to go back home; they realized that they could not find anyone who knew what absolute happiness is. On their way home, shortly before they approached the palace, they heard a joyous melody. A person was singing freely, and they sensed that he was really happy.

They turned their horses in the direction of the song and they saw a drunken man, reeling back and forth with a huge smile on his face. "Are you happy," they asked him. "I am the happiest person in the world," he answered. "Absolutely happy?" "Yes. I have not a care on my mind."

And they saw that it was true. He did not worry; he had no anxieties nor fears. They realized that this was the man they were looking for. They told him, "Sir, we need your shirt. The king is sick, but the healer said that if he puts on the shirt of a happy man, he will be healed. Lend us your shirt for a short while. We promise that you will be amply rewarded."

The man replied, "I would be happy to help the king, and I do not need his rewards. But there is one problem. I do not own a shirt."

The point of the story is: because he does not own a shirt — that is why he is the happiest person in the world.

On the one hand, the story looks good. It tells you that many of us are so concerned with who we are and what we have that we can never really let loose and be happy. Our self-concern ties us down and prevents us from experiencing real happiness.

There is a pithy truth to this message. But beneath the surface, there is something negative here. This person has nothing, no purpose, no goal in life, nothing that he is working for, nothing to look forward to. It is true that he has nothing holding him back from being happy. But he also has no genuine source of happiness; his life is empty.

When a person has a goal to achieve — be it a self-oriented goal like making money or a more altruistic goal like teaching or helping others — he will define his happiness in terms of his achievement of his goal. There are times when he will be successful, and other times when he will fail. Since life has its ups and downs, he will never be absolutely happy. Why does the drunkard in our story think that he is so happy? Because he has absolutely nothing at all that bothers him. But that is tragic, not happy.

There has never been an animal who has gone to a psychologist and complained that he feels unfulfilled, that he has not accomplished enough. An animal does not think like that. Take a dog: he gets up in the morning, barks a little, rolls around on his back, runs around, eats some food, goes to sleep, plays, sleeps again, and gets up for more the next day. This goes on year after year. It is fine for a dog; his nature does not demand anything more of him. He will never feel unfulfilled.

A human being, however, is different. He has a brain and a soul, and unless he taps their potential he will never be satisfied. The drunk feels happy because he has no shirt, meaning he has nothing to himself. But this is not real happiness. In Hebrew, we call this *holelus* (frivolity), not *simchah* (joy). It is an animal form of satisfaction, where the person does not live up to his potential.

Can we combine *simchah* and responsibility? Is it possible to have purpose and direction, and at the same time to let loose and feel free?

Yes. This is the type of happiness that comes from *kabbalas ol,* accepting G-d's yoke. On the one hand, a person lets go of his self-consciousness, but he does not sink into emptiness; he connects to a force that is much higher than himself. Both the letting go and the connection are sources of *simchah.*

Let us return to the analogy used in the story. Happiness comes from "not having a shirt of your own"; being able to rise above one's self-concerns. The question is, however, does one, like the drunkard, walk around naked — i.e., discard one's human potential? Or does one — as does a master of *kabbalas ol* — continue wearing the shirt, but transfer ownership of it to G-d?

The drunkard's happiness is destructive; it ruins his ability to build a life for himself and the people close to him. True joy involves self-transcendence — and more than that, the establishment of a connection to one's inner G-dly core. This builds personal strength. A person who experiences real happiness grows and becomes able to overcome personal limitations that had previously hampered him. He is open and friendly with others, and imbues them with joy as well. He radiates trust in G-d and appreciation for all the good He grants us.

In other words, there is a type of joy that destroys a person, and there is a type of joy that makes a person even stronger than he was before. When a person lets go of himself without direction, it is destructive. Imagine taking your hands off the steering wheel while speeding down a busy highway. The path of life requires as much attention as does any road.

But then there are times where we transfer control, like a flyer going into automatic pilot. Although we have taken our hands off the wheel, we have not stopped thinking about the direction of the flight. It is just that Someone else is doing the steering. And taking our hands off the wheel is not a proper analogy, because in actual life, our hands are on the wheel; we must take responsibility for our lives. And yet, through observing the Torah and its *mitzvos,* we follow a lifestyle that leads to self-transcendence.

A person who does not believe in G-d and does not recognize the G-dly element within his being can never experience true joy. He is either wrapped up in himself or living a life of emptiness. He has no other alternative because he is not aware of anything beyond his own self.

When, by contrast, a person recognizes G-d and realizes that G-d lies at the core of his own being, he can truly let go of himself. And then he can feel genuine happiness.

Holelus means letting go by becoming less than what one really is. The person forgets about himself and about anything that has meaning, content and purpose. In the extreme, this means becoming drunk, or taking drugs that rob one of control. But it has far more common expressions. A person thinks that the only way he can be happy is by forgetting about everything but the sensory pleasure he is receiving at the time. He lives for the moment.

This can be very destructive, for when a person ignores responsibility, he is likely to hurt himself, his family and the people around him.

Simchah, joy, also involves letting go, but it is a very different type of letting go. One does not lose control — one transfers control. When a person experiences true joy, he lets go of himself, but he connects to something higher, G-d. He lets go of his petty ego and makes it possible for a dimension of his identity that is far deeper and far truer to surface.

This is one of the reasons *simchah* is considered a high level of Divine service. For this selfless connection with G-d — over and above all the advantages one gains by avoiding depression — is a goal for which we should all strive.

That is what *Shabbos* and the holidays are all about. On these days, we rise above all humdrum worldly experience and sense true joy.

Have you ever seen people singing and dancing for hours and hours on Simchas Torah? The people who are celebrating are humans, not angels. They each have their own array of worries and troubles. But on Simchas Torah they are not concerned with these matters at all. They are not thinking of themselves. As they sing and dance, they are connecting to a deeper dimension that exists within their being. That is where the *simchah* comes from.

The Previous Rebbe used to say[2] that on Simchas Torah, the Torah itself wants to dance. However, since a Torah scroll has no feet, the Jews must function as its feet and carry it around the reader's platform.

This analogy enables us to understand why a person can be so happy on Simchas Torah. Because he has gone beyond his own identity, he is no more than the Torah's feet, and he can rejoice with complete abandon. And yet, his life will be filled with the meaning and purpose that stems from the Torah he is carrying.

───────────────

2. *Sefer HaSichos* 5704, p. 36.

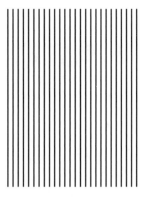

Chapter Eleven
SIMCHAH: A DYNAMIC OF EMPOWERMENT

Joy is important, not only as the antithesis of depression, but as a fundamental element of our Divine service in its own right. Just as the love of G-d and the fear of G-d are necessary for our Divine service to be complete, so too, joy is essential to our spiritual development. All the *mitzvos* that a person performs, and everything that he does as an expression of his connection to G-d, should be inspired with joy.

This is reflected in Psalms, which tells us:[1] "Serve G-d with joy; come before Him in celebration" — celebration being a medium that allows us to come before G-d and feel His presence. The *Rambam* clearly spells out this concept, writing:[2]

> The happiness with which a person should rejoice in the fulfillment of the *mitzvos* and the love of G-d... is a great service.... There is no greatness or honor other than celebrating before G-d.

1. 100:2.
2. *Mishneh Torah, Hilchos Lulav* 8:15.

Similarly, with regard to prophecy, the *Rambam* mentions[3] several prerequisites for prophecy that reflect the epitome of personal development: "Prophecy is bestowed only upon a very wise sage of a strong character, who is never overcome by his natural inclinations in any regard. Instead, with his mind he overcomes his natural inclinations at all times."

Nevertheless, he emphasizes[4] that "prophecy cannot rest on a person when he is sad and languid, but only when he is happy." The experience of prophecy involves the Divine Presence manifesting itself within a person, and this is possible only when the person is happy.

This concept is also reflected with regard to the *Beis HaMikdash,* the permanent home for G-d's Presence. It is written,[5] "Strength and gladness are in His place." His place, the *Beis HaMikdash*, was characterized by happiness, as evidenced by the joyous songs that the Levites would sing and play on their instruments.

Similarly, with regard to time: *Shabbos,* the holiest day of the week, and the festivals, days set aside for their holiness, are days of happiness and rejoicing, for happiness brings us closer to G-d.

Not only is *simchah* an important feature in a Jew's service of G-d, but in a sense, serving G-d with *simchah* can be considered higher than all other paths of Divine service. Let us share a story told about Rabbi Levi Yitzchok of Berditchev. Once, on the day before Yom Kippur, a Jewish innkeeper living near Berditchev was arrested by the landowner on whose property the Jew's inn was located.

The Jew had not paid his rent for a long period of time. He was not trying to steal; he just did not have the money. Business was not that good; he had a large family; and on

---

3. *Mishneh Torah, Hilchos Yesodei HaTorah* 7:1.
4. *Ibid.:4.*
5. *I Chronicles* 16:27.

the day that the rent was due, he simply did not have the money.

In those days, the landowners were very powerful. In their own territories, they ruled like kings. So after waiting several days for his money and issuing a number of warnings, the landowner locked up this Jewish innkeeper and his family on the day before Yom Kippur. He told the Jewish community that unless they present him with the overdue rent — 300 rubles, no small sum of money in those days — the family would rot away in a dungeon for the rest of their lives.

One of the greatest *mitzvos* is *pidyon sh'vuyim,* the redemption of captives. And so, one of the *chassidim* in Berditchev took it upon himself to collect the money to redeem this family. Although the sum was well beyond his means, he wanted to make this effort because he knew that the lives of the family depended on it. They had no one else to help them, and unless he was able to amass the money, they would stay in the landowner's dungeon until they died.

He began collecting. Since it was the day before Yom Kippur, the people were especially sensitive and gave generously. But they did not give enough. It is not that they did not want to — just as the innkeeper had not had the money to pay his rent, they also did not have that much to give. And so, after collecting for several hours, the man had managed to gather less than fifty rubles.

He knew he needed three hundred, and he realized that at this pace he would never get the money before Yom Kippur and might never get the money at all. He decided to take a rasher course of action, and headed to the neighborhood where the free-thinking Jews lived. These were younger people, who worked with the non-Jewish landlords. They were wealthier, but their concern for their fellow Jews and for Jewish practice was less. Still, it was the day before Yom Kippur, and there would be no better time to approach them.

When he reached that neighborhood, he saw a hall filled with many people. There were Jews sitting there gambling, playing cards. The fact that in a few hours Jews all over the world would be saying *Kol Nidrei* did not appear to interest them. They were interested in playing cards, drinking vodka and gambling.

The *chassid* saw that the tables were filled with money. On any one of the tables there was enough money to redeem the family. He approached one of the tables and told the people, "Tonight is Yom Kippur, the time when G-d forgives everyone. Why not prepare for the day? I have something constructive for you to do with your money. A family is in terrible need. Instead of wasting your money gambling, give it away for a good purpose."

At first, the people just ignored him. But the *chassid* was persistent. Finally, one of them told him, "You know what? You see this vodka standing here on the table? It is *finif un ninesiker*." *Finif un ninesiker* means 95%. The bottle was 95% alcohol. That is not 95 proof, that is 190 proof. The man filled an ordinary drinking glass and told him, "If you drink a glass of this *finif un ninesiker*, we will collect 100 rubles for your cause from our table alone."

The reaction of the *chassid* was, "How can I drink a glass of whisky that is 190 proof? In a couple of hours, it will be *Kol Nidrei*. After a full glass of this, I will be finished; there is no way I will be able to concentrate on my prayers." But then a second thought came to his mind, "If they give me a hundred rubles, I will have a third of the amount I need to save this family. What should I be concerned with? Having a more spiritual Yom Kippur myself or doing everything I can to save the family? Who knows how long it will take to collect one hundred rubles any other way?" And so, he made the decision to drink the glass of vodka.

He downed the glass; and the gamblers kept their word and gave him the money. Afterwards, he wobbled over to the next table and spoke to the people, "You see your friends, they just gave me a 100 rubles to help a poor family. Why do you not do the same?"

The people told him, "You know what? We will do the same, but you will have to do the same, too. If you drink another glass of *finif un ninesiker*, we will also give you 100 rubles."

The *chassid* began to plead with them, "Please, tonight is *Kol Nidrei*. As it is, I am going to be dizzy tonight, but if I drink another glass, I am just going to be out. You are going to give me the money anyway, so why make me do this?"

But the people demanded their entertainment. "Listen, either drink it or good-bye." Again the *chassid* thought, "What is more important: my spiritual experience on *Yom Kippur* or the fact that I can get this family out of the dungeon earlier?" He did not have to think long. His entire life was directed towards others, not to himself. And so he gave them their entertainment and drank the glass of vodka. They gave him the hundred rubles, and everyone was happy.

Afterwards, he wobbled over to a third table and asked them whether they would contribute to the cause. He explained that now he needed less than a hundred rubles. It was just hours before Yom Kippur, and they could make it possible for a poor family to spend the holiday outside a dungeon.

They were not interested in his explanations, but they were prepared to continue the fun. So they made him the same offer: one hundred rubles for a glass of *finif un ninesiker*. He did not have to think much at all. Particularly after two glasses of vodka, it was very clear to him: "Forget about a more spiritual Yom Kippur; think about the family. With this glass, you can get them out today." He drank the third glass and they gave him the 100 rubles. Now he had all the money he needed to get the family out.

He asked the gamblers a favor, "Please, can someone help me get over to the home of this landowner so that I can give him the money?" The spirit of Yom Kippur must have indeed been in the air, for one of the gamblers excused himself from his company and drove the *chassid* to the landowner's home in his carriage.

The landowner was not happy to see a drunken man at his door, but he was very happy to get his three hundred rubles. After counting the money, he ordered that the family be released. Naturally, they were ecstatic. The innkeeper ran over to the *chassid* and hugged him, thanking him profusely. The *chassid* was not interested in receiving thanks; he did not see anything special in what he had done. He asked the innkeeper one favor. "I will not be able to get to the *shul* by myself. Could you help get me there?"

Needless to say, the innkeeper obliged and brought the *chassid* to the *shul*. There he lay down on one of the benches. He knew that he would not be able to pray, but he wanted at least to sleep in the atmosphere of Yom Kippur.

Soon people started coming to *shul* for *Kol Nidrei*. Everyone took a book of *Tehillim* in hand and prayed. As the din of their prayers began to rise, the *chassid* was aroused. He looked up and saw the ark open and people taking out Torah scrolls. Although this is also done before the *Kol Nidrei* prayers, the most normal association a person would have with Torah scrolls being taken out at night, particularly when he is intoxicated, is the celebration of Simchas Torah.

And so our *chassid* jumped up from his bench, ran up to the *bimah*, the platform on which everyone was standing, and began shouting *"Atah Horeisa,"* the prayer recited before the Simchas Torah *Hakkofos*. Everyone looked at him in amazement. "What is he doing? Doesn't he know tonight is Yom Kippur?! In a few moments we will be reciting *Kol Nidrei*. What kind of joke is he playing? Is he drunk?" They were about to grab him and throw him out of the *shul*.

But the Rebbe, R. Levi Yitzchok of Berditchev turned around and said, "Leave him alone. He has the right to do what he is doing." R. Levi Yitzchok was a *tzaddik,* a completely righteous and spiritual person. He knew everything the *chassid* had gone through.

He began to explain to the congregation that the holidays of Tishrei follow in sequence. It is not mere coincidence that Rosh HaShanah is followed by Yom Kippur, and then by Sukkos, Shemini Atzeres, and Simchas Torah. A spiritual initiative begins on Rosh HaShanah and continues and intensifies until it reaches its peak on Simchas Torah.

"This person," he said, pointing to the drunken *chassid,* "has just displayed tremendous *mesirus nefesh* (self-sacrifice). He sacrificed his Yom Kippur experience to save a Jewish family. But he did not give up Yom Kippur; he sprang over it. His self-sacrifice enabled him to bypass all the intermediate levels and reach the level of Simchas Torah, the zenith of our Divine service throughout Tishrei."

There are a lot of things we can learn from this story. One of the concepts relates to the subject of our discussion, the preeminence of the service of *simchah,* joy. As we explained, the holidays of the month of Tishrei are like a spiritual ladder, with each holiday serving as a stepping stone to the next. What is the last holiday, the highest rung reached during the month? Simchas Torah.

On Simchas Torah, we do not make a special increase in the time we spend studying; basically, what we do is sing and dance with the Torah scrolls. *Simchah,* joy, is the main feature of this holiday.

Although Rosh HaShanah and Yom Kippur are the Days of Awe — the holiest days of the year — Simchas Torah is the climax of the Tishrei experience, indicating that serving G-d with joy is the highest rung on this ladder of spiritual connection to G-d.

This may be difficult for us to understand: On Rosh HaShanah and Yom Kippur, a person must seek to penetrate to his spiritual core and arouse the G-dliness that lies at the essence of his being. We have no difficulty understanding that this is a powerful spiritual experience. It is much harder to understand that singing and dancing are spiritual, and indeed so spiritual that the rejoicing of Simchas Torah surpasses the soul-stirring prayers of Rosh HaShanah and Yom Kippur.

The resolution of this difficulty depends on a fundamental concept: that the essence of the Jews' connection to G-d is *bittul*, selflessness, feeling at one with G-d. *Bittul* means not seeing oneself as a separate, independent entity, and G-d as another separate, independent entity, but rather recognizing that all existence — including one's own self — is a manifestation and an expression of G-dliness.

This changes a person's conception of who he is. Instead of understanding his true self as his individual identity, he appreciates his soul, the G-dliness that is within him. This also gives us a new understanding of *mitzvos*: every *mitzvah* that we perform brings this inner oneness to the surface and intensifies it. Instead of being a checklist of how many *mitzvos* we have performed and how much Torah we have studied, our Divine service becomes a process leading us away from *yeshus*, the awareness of ourselves as an independent entity, bringing us to *bittul*, selfless union with G-d.

In a certain way, *simchah* is the strongest, most powerful demonstration of this oneness. When a person is *b'simchah*, he rises above self-concern; he does not think of himself at all. He is able to recognize that there is something deeper and greater beyond him — G-d. And he can become aware that G-dliness is within him.

Simchah allows for the most complete level of connection to G-d. When a person does a good deed, he does not necessarily transcend his ego. For example, when a person gives charity, it is true that he is giving away his money, but he may not be letting go entirely. Often the person will feel satisfaction at having given. His sense of *self* still figures into the equation.

The same is true for all the other *mitzvos;* they do not necessarily take a person totally beyond himself. This can even be true of the *mitzvah* of loving G-d. Although this love should be an actual feeling of connection — not merely an abstract conception — just as in every relationship, the person involved feels his own identity.

In contrast, *simchah,* by definition, requires a person to go beyond himself. The only way a person can truly experience *simchah* is if he completely and totally lets go of himself. Unless he is willing to surrender himself in this manner, he will always have things that are weighing him down. As long as a person thinks about himself, his concerns — whether material or spiritual — will prevent him from being *b'simchah.* Only when a person leaves his *self* behind and connects to G-d can he experience true joy.

This relates to the renowned statement of our Rabbis,[6] *simchah poretz geder,* "joy breaks through barriers." When a person is happy, his joy fills him with energy and enables him to break through any barriers that stand in his way.

For this reason, we find that when people are happy, they can overcome certain weaknesses with which they could not deal under ordinary circumstances. Everyone has limitations and weaknesses that prevent him from making real progress. Being *b'simchah* enables him to go beyond those weaknesses. Since *simchah* brings out the deeper and true dimension of one's identity, the essence is not confined to the limitations of one's ego.

We see examples of this in history. One of the things kings would do on the day of their coronation or at a royal wedding was to pardon prisoners. What connection does pardoning prisoners have with a wedding or a coronation? The idea is that these are times that the king is *b'simchah,* and so the blocks created by the prisoner's past conduct no longer exist for him. Yes, the prisoner did something wrong,

6.   *Sefer HaMaamarim 5657,* p. 223ff.

but when there is happiness in the air, there can be no obstacles hindering the inner relationship a king shares with his subjects. And therefore he pardons them.

Simchah generates energy; it pushes us forward and gives us a sense of productivity and growth. It does not mean that we will merely forget about our problems and pretend they do not exist. It means that we are given new energies that enable us to overcome any problems that we may confront.

The medical community is also beginning to recognize the power of joy. Researchers have discovered that even physiological problems and diseases can be more easily overcome with *simchah*. They call it "healing with laughter." There are stories of people who had cancer ר"ל for which they had been treated without success. Nevertheless, over time, when these people were put into an intensely joyous frame of mind, their cancer disappeared!

Often the body possesses the resources to heal itself, but depression hampers the body and prevents these resources from working. *Simchah,* by contrast, stimulates energy and gives the body the opportunity to overcome infirmity.

Surely, this concept applies with regard to the functioning of our minds and hearts. *Simchah* does not merely transfer our attention away from our difficulties; it arouses unlimited inner energy that enables us to break through problems, weaknesses and limitations. It stirs our creativity and gives us the potential to live a productive life, continually advancing to higher peaks.

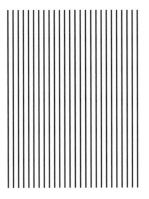

Chapter Twelve
A LIGHTNING ROD TO THE SPIRITUAL REALMS

The positive potential of *simchah* is highlighted by the Maggid of Mezeritch's interpretation[1] of the teaching in *Pirkei Avos:*[2] "Know what is above you." Literally, the *Mishnah* is teaching us always to be conscious that, allegorically speaking, in the spiritual realms there exists an eye that sees everything we do, an ear that hears everything we say, and a hand that records everything that takes place.

The Maggid of Mezeritch extended the meaning of this teaching. He would say: "Know that everything above" — all that transpires in the spiritual realm — is "from you," dependent on your conduct. Each of us influences what goes on in the spiritual realm. And so, when a person is happy, he not only lifts the spirits of the people around him, but he generates joy in the spiritual realm as well.

Let us explain the dynamics at work: One of the most fundamental concepts discussed in the *Kabbalah* and in

---

1. Cited in *Or HaTorah al Aggados Chazal*, p. 112b.
2. 2:1; See *In the Paths of Our Fathers*, p. 43 (Kehot, N.Y., 1994).

Chassidic philosophy is the interrelationship between the spiritual realm and our material reality. The *Zohar*[3] states that our material world parallels the spiritual realm. It is like a mirror reflecting an object or person before it. When one sees a person moving a hand in the mirror, one realizes that standing in front of the mirror is an actual person who is moving his hand. Even when we cannot see the person himself, the image in the mirror is sufficient.

Similar concepts apply with regard to the interrelation between the physical and spiritual realms. Our physical realm mirrors spiritual reality. Everything taking place on our plane has a parallel within — and gives us an understanding of — the workings of spiritual existence. Although we may not be directly conscious of spiritual reality, we can understand many things about it from the parallels we see in our world.

This concept also has a deeper dimension. When we are speaking of a mirror and a person, we are talking about two separate, unrelated entities; one merely reflects the other. With regard to the spiritual and the physical, it is not that the spiritual realm is one form of existence and the physical realm another, with G-d creating them to correspond to each other. In this instance, the two are more closely related. Our material existence is merely an extension of the spiritual.

We do not have a proper analogy to illustrate this. One of the closest examples we have is the relationship between the soul and the body. Our Sages tell us[4] that just as the soul fills up the body, G-d fills up the world. Therefore, if we want to develop a better understanding of the interaction between G-d and the world — or in different words, the spiritual realm and the physical realm — we can focus on the relationship between the body and the soul, the *neshamah* and the *guf*.

---

3.   I, 38a, 205b; c.f. *Berachos* 58a; *Zohar* I, 197a, III, 176b.
4.   *Berachos* 10a.

The activity of a person's soul is reflected in his body. If a person is anxious, you can tell by looking at him. One look at his eyes and his facial expression tells the whole story. The same is true when he is angry and when he is sad. And surely this is true when he is happy. When a person is truly *b'simchah*, his face radiates joy. For what a person experiences internally expresses itself in his physical form.

It has to be this way. The soul and the body function as a single entity. Although they have different sources, as long as a person is alive, his body and his soul share a single identity, and the body expresses what is happening within the person's soul.

A similar concept applies with regard to the interaction between the spiritual realm and the physical realm. When we see something happening in the physical realm — for example, it is raining — what we are seeing is, in essence, a reflection of what is taking place in the spiritual realm. In the spiritual realm, there is a great outpouring of kindness, and that becomes manifest in our world as rain.

And this holds true for all the events that take place in our world — a snowfall, a wind, an earthquake. From the most unusual to the most mundane, everything that occurs in our world is a result — and a reflection — of something that is taking place in the spiritual realm.

There is, however, a dual nature to the dynamic of causation. Just as what happens in our material realm is a result of what is taking place in the spiritual realm, what takes place in the spiritual realm can be determined by the events of our world. This is the meaning of the teaching of the Maggid of Mezeritch mentioned above. He explained that the *Mishnah* in *Pirkei Avos* is telling us to: "Know that what is above" — the goings on in the spiritual realm — "is from you" — dependent on our conduct. We mortals determine the nature of the influences active in the spiritual realm.

Why does man have this potential? Because "man was created in the image of G-d."[5] Needless to say, this does not mean that G-d has the same physical form as man; G-d is infinite and He has no body or shape whatsoever.[6] *Chassidus* and *Kabbalah*, nevertheless, explain that there is a spiritual counterpart to all our bodily features. G-d does not possess eyes, but He possesses a means of perception that operates — in a more complete way than we could possibly comprehend — in a manner comparable to our power of sight. He does not possess a mouth, but He possesses a means of expression that corresponds to our power of speech. Similarly, every element of our being has its counterpart in the spiritual realm.

And so, when we move our hands, we are also activating the spiritual counterpart of our hands. Everything we do — all of our activities and everything that goes on in our lives in this physical realm — has an effect in the spiritual world.

In particular, there are three phases in this cycle: our deeds, the effect that activity has in the spiritual realm, and the reflection of the activity within the spiritual realm in our material world.

For example, when someone is not well, G-d forbid, and a friend decides to give charity in his merit, the friend's gift activates G-d's attribute of *chessed* (kindness) in the spiritual realm. This in turn becomes manifest in our world in the improvement of the sick person's condition.

The Baal Shem Tov explains a similar idea,[7] commenting on the verse,[8] "G-d is your shadow." Literally, the verse tells us that just as a shadow protects us from the sun, G-d shields us. The Baal Shem Tov, however, offers an extended interpretation, explaining that just as a shadow mirrors a person's actions, the nature of the influence that flows from

---

5. *Genesis* 1:27.
6. See *Rambam, Mishneh Torah, Hilchos Yesodei HaTorah* 1:7-12.
7. *Keser Shem Tov, Hosafos* 60.
8. *Tehillim* 121:5.

G-d to the world will be a reflection of the nature of our activities.

This same idea is reflected in the Maggid's interpretation of the *Mishnah*, "Know what is above you," that "what is above" is dependent on "you." Everything that happens in the spiritual realm is determined by our behavior, because whatever we do activates the counterpart in the spiritual realm. And that spiritual activity brings about changes in our world. When I show compassion to another person, that motivates G-d to show compassion.

Let us take another example of this idea. When two people marry, their union reflects the creation of a similar bond in the spiritual realm. For within the spiritual realm, there are two aspects: one referred to as *Malchus,* which reflects the feminine dimension, and another, referred to as *Zaer Anpin,* which reflects the masculine dimension. When a man and woman marry, they bring about a union between these attributes in the spiritual realm. This union, in turn, encourages the flow of positive influence to our material world.

Similar concepts apply with regard to speech. Everything said in our realm activates a counterpart in the spiritual realm. So when we say good things, positive influences are generated in the spiritual realm. And if, G-d forbid, we say unfavorable things, negative influences are generated.

This is one of the explanations of our Sages' statement,[9] "Do not regard the blessing of an ordinary person lightheartedly." We know that blessings given by a *tzaddik,* a righteous person, can bring about miraculous changes in our lives. But the truth is that whenever anyone gives a blessing, the blessing has power. For the person's statements create effects not only in our world, but in the spiritual realm. When he speaks words of blessing, he is actually generating

---

9.   *Berachos* 7a.

a blessing in the spiritual realm. And that blessing can effect change in our world.

[The converse is also true. And for this reason, the Torah forbids cursing another person. For this can also, Heaven forbid, have an effect.]

Our thoughts also effect changes in the spiritual realm. In this world, thought has no apparent effect, but the dynamic of spiritual causation is such that every expression of our being — be it thought, speech, or action — creates a spiritual effect. And that spiritual effect can later bring about changes in our world. Indeed, we find that intense thought about another person has often produced very positive effects.[10]

There was once a *chassid* whose son was very ill. After a prolonged illness, the physicians finally told him that there was no hope. There was nothing more they could do; they did not know if the child would live.

The *chassid* was devastated. He hurried to Lubavitch and approached the Tzemach Tzedek, the third Lubavitcher Rebbe. Overcome with grief, he could barely mouth his request for a blessing.

The Rebbe answered him briefly in Yiddish: *Tracht gut, vet zein gut.* "Think positively, and the outcome will be good."[11]

As the *chassid* walked out of the Rebbe's room, he pulled himself together. He put himself in a state of mind that radiated utter confidence. He knew G-d could help him and cure his son. And he believed that this would happen.

When he came home, he was told that there had been a sudden change in his son's condition. The physicians had no explanation, but the child had definitely taken a turn for the

10. *Likkutei Dibburim*, Vol. I, p. 6 (English translation).
11. See *Sefer HaSichos 5687*, p. 113 and sources cited there; explained in *Likkutei Sichos, Parshas Shemos 5751*.

better. When the *chassid* inquired, he was told that the change took place at exactly the time that he visited the Rebbe.

The story shows us that thinking positively produces two effects:

a) when a person is in high spirits, he functions better; and

b) thinking positively itself brings about positive change. By envisioning good in one's mind, one creates positive spiritual influence that enables that picture to materialize.

This is the basis of the *Chassidic* explanation of one of the most fundamental principles of Judaism, *bitochon. Bitochon* means confidence and trust that G-d will help. That G-d can help us at any given time is a point of faith, and one that is very easy to accept. After all, if He is G-d, He is capable of doing anything He wants. *Bitochon* means more than that; it expresses our trust and confidence that He will actually help.

Bitochon is not euphoric escapism; it does not absolve an individual of taking responsibility for his future, and acting accordingly. It means that as a person acts, he realizes that his efforts are dependent on G-d's providence, and he relies on G-d and trusts Him totally.

Besides giving a person the confidence and inner strength to face challenges, this approach also generates positive Divine influence. When a person trusts and relies on G-d, G-d creates situations that will allow him to use his energies in positive and beneficial ways.[12] Our positive thoughts serve as catalysts that promote favorable circumstances for us.

Now we can appreciate the importance of *simchah*. When a person is genuinely happy and sees things in a positive

---

12. See *Sefer HaIkkarim*, Discourse 4, Chapter 47.

way, he creates *simchah* in the spiritual realm. For "everything that happens above is dependent on you."

The joy that is activated in the spiritual realm is not self-contained, but flows outward, bringing joy to many others in our world. When we are *b'simchah*, in both a physical and spiritual way, we bring joy to ourselves, our families, and all the people around us.

As we explained in the previous chapter, this joy is not a passive potential. On the contrary, "joy breaks through barriers," destroying all the obstacles and difficulties that may present themselves.

When a person is happy, he stands above all his personal limitations and weaknesses. He can do things that he ordinarily could not do. He can forgive his worst enemy. His joy generates inner energy that breaks through and shatters any barrier that stands in his way.

When a person creates joy in the spiritual realm, the same thing happens. In the spiritual realm, there are also limitations and barriers, for G-d has chosen to establish a natural order through which He controls our world. Just as there are rules of nature that govern the physical world around us, there are principles of causality that govern the effects produced by our conduct. For as above, everything we do generates an effect in the spiritual realm that in turn produces an effect within our world. On the most general level, these rules follow the following principle:[13] When a person does good, he receives benefits that enable him to continue in this path. If he fails to do good, he will suffer difficulties that make it obvious to him that he should change his ways. These are the patterns of causation that G-d chose to establish in the spiritual realm.

Nevertheless, when a person is *b'simchah*, he creates joy in the spiritual realm; G-d Himself is, so to speak, also *b'simchah*. This causes G-d to reveal a transcendent dimen-

---

13. See *Rambam, Hilchos Teshuvah* 9:1.

sion that is not bound by the laws of causation mentioned above. In simple terms, this means that G-d will give great blessings and make positive things happen, even though normally these blessings would not be granted.

When, G-d forbid, there is a situation where something is not going right, we must realize that this is a result of the laws of causation that G-d established. We must, however, also realize that by radiating *simchah*, we can awaken *simchah* above, and effect a radical change in the situation before us.

This demonstrates the power our joy possesses. With *simchah* we can change the makeup of the spiritual realm, and in this manner, bring blessing and all forms of good to ourselves, our families, and to the entire Jewish people.

∞

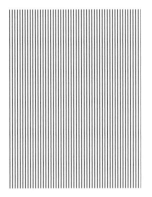

Selections from the *Sichos* of
Shabbos Parshas Ki Seitzei, 5748
BRINGING *MASHIACH* WITH HAPPINESS

(There is no way that a treatment of the *Chassidic* conception of joy could be complete without referring to this classic *sichah* delivered by the Lubavitcher Rebbe in 1988. In its original form, the *sichah* discusses concepts related to the date on which it was delivered, the fourteenth of the month of Elul: the dates of the weddings of the Previous Rebbe and the Rebbe Rashab to which it shares proximity; the significance of the years 5748 and 5749 (1988 and 1989); and others. We have omitted those portions, focusing on the dimensions of the *sichah* which are general in nature.)

The concept of *simchah* shares a connection to the Future Redemption. For it is in the Era of the Redemption that we will experience the consummate level of *simchah*. At that time, all undesirable influences will be negated as reflected in the verse,[1] "And G-d will wipe away tears from every face." Indeed, all the negative influences will be transformed into good.[2]

---

1.   *Isaiah* 25:8.
2.   As evident from the *Rambam's* ruling (at the conclusion of *Hilchos Taanios* in the *Mishneh Torah*): "In the future, all these [commemorative] fasts will be negated

This will greatly increase the *simchah* we will experience, enabling it to reach consummate perfection. Therefore the returnees to *Eretz Yisrael* are described[3] as being "crowned with eternal joy." The relation between the concepts of *simchah* and Redemption is alluded to by the fact that the roots of the words *simchah* (שמחה) and *Mashiach* (משיח)[4] share the same three letters שמח.

To explain the connection between the two: *Simchah* breaks through (*poretzes* in Hebrew) all barriers.[5] This is also the nature of *Mashiach,* who is a descendant of Peretz,[6] and is referred to as *haporetz,* "the one who breaks through," as it is written,[7] "The one who breaks through will ascend before them." For *Mashiach* will break through all barriers and limitations.

On the verse,[8] "Zion — there are none who seek her out," our Sages[9] comment, "This indicates that one should seek her out," implying that we must demand the Redemption. Similarly, we must seek out joy, including the ultimate joy, the joy of the Redemption. We must demand that G-d grant us the consummate joy of the Era of the Redemption.

I, therefore, offer the following suggestion and request: that we increase our rejoicing with the intent of actually bringing *Mashiach* and the true and ultimate Redemption.

Throughout the years of exile, the Jewish people have longed for the Redemption and prayed for it earnestly every day. Surely this applies to the *tzaddikim,* and the *nesi'im* of the Jewish people who had an overwhelmingly powerful

---

in the Era of the *Mashiach.* Moreover, they will then become festivals, and days of rejoicing and joy."

3. *Yeshayahu* 35:10, 51:11.
4. The ה of the word שמחה alludes to the concept of extension and expansion (as explained in *Iggeres HaTeshuvah,* ch. 4), while the י of the word משיח refers to the fact that *Mashiach* reflects the essential point of *Chochmah.* It can be explained that *simchah* has the potential to expand and reveal the influence of *Mashiach.*
5. See the series of discourses entitled *Samach Tisamach,* 5657.
6. See the conclusion of the Book of Ruth.
7. *Michah* 2:13.
8. *Yirmeyahu* 30:17.
9. *Rosh HaShanah* 31a.

desire for *Mashiach*. Indeed, as related in the annals of our national history, some[10] actually sacrificed their lives to force *Mashiach* to come earlier (although there is a specific warning against doing so).[11]

Nevertheless, these earlier activities cannot be compared to the storm for the coming of the Redemption aroused by the Previous Rebbe with his cry (printed[12] more than forty years ago): *L'alter leteshuvah, l'alter legeulah*, "Immediately to *teshuvah*; immediately to Redemption."[13] And his intent with the word "immediately" was simple: at once, straight-away.

Moreover, this is not considered as forcing the Redemption to come before its time. For the time of the Redemption has arrived. As the Previous Rebbe stated many times: all the service necessary has been completed; all that is necessary is to polish the buttons,[14] and to await *Mashiach's* coming.

To explain in a more specific manner: For several generations prior to the Previous Rebbe, special efforts were made to bring about *Mashiach's* coming, including — and with a special emphasis on — the revelation of the teachings

---

10. E.g., R. Yosef DiLorino and the Seer of Lublin.

11. See *Kesuvos* 111a and *Rashi's* commentary. It can be explained that the charge against trying to force the Redemption to come before its time is necessary because of the great desire the Jewish people have for the Redemption. So powerful is their desire, that it is necessary to warn them not to try to bring the Redemption before its time.

12. In the *Kol Korei* (announcement) published in *HaKeriah VehaKedushah* (Sivan-Tammuz, 5701; Elul, 5702).

13. Within the expression itself, the emphasis is on "Immediately to Redemption" as reflected by the fact that "Immediately to Redemption" is mentioned several times in the announcement alone, without the preface "Immediately to *teshuvah*." "Immediately to *teshuvah*" is necessary only as a preface for Redemption, as the *Rambam* writes (*Mishneh Torah, Hilchos Teshuvah* 7:5): "The Torah has promised that ultimately, at the conclusion of its exile, Israel will turn to G-d in *teshuvah* and immediately afterwards, [the nation] will be redeemed."

14. See *Sichos Simchas Torah*, 5689.

[Publisher's note: The Rebbe delivered this *sichah* in 5748 (1988). Subsequently, from the summer of 5751 (1991) onward, he was wont to say, "the buttons are already polished," i.e., this final stage of Divine service has also been completed.

of *Chassidus* by the Baal Shem Tov. For in reply to the Baal Shem Tov's question, "When are you coming?" *Mashiach* answered, "When the wellsprings of your teachings spread outward."[15]

Afterwards, these teachings were expanded and developed through the teachings of *Chabad* which enabled them to be understood and grasped within the context of our intellectual powers.[16] To cite the analogy offered by the Alter Rebbe:[17] the precious stone in the king's crown has been crushed and mixed with water so that it can be poured into the mouth of the king's son to save his life.

From generation to generation, the *Rebbeim* have continued and expanded the efforts to spread the wellsprings of *Chassidus* outward. These efforts reached their zenith in the time of the Previous Rebbe[18] who spread these teachings outward in an incomparable manner, reaching out to each and every locale throughout the world, extending the wellsprings of *Chassidus* to the furthest possible peripheries. Similarly, his efforts included the translation of *Chassidic* texts (including deeper concepts in *Chassidus*) into foreign languages.[19] He did not remain content with a translation into Yiddish, the language spoken by most of the Jews of his

15. See the renowned letter of the Baal Shem Tov printed at the beginning of *Kesser Shem Tov.*

16. To refer to the analogy of a wellspring: a spring often flows in droplets, although these drops have great power, as reflected in the law (*Hilchos Mikvaos* 9:8) that a drop of water from a spring, regardless of its size, is able to restore an object to a state of ritual purity. Nevertheless, through the teachings of *Chabad*, these wellsprings have been expanded and broadened.

17. *HaTamim*, Vol. II, p. 49.

18. The connection between the Previous Rebbe and the spreading of the wellsprings of *Chassidus* is reflected in the establishment of the Lubavitcher *Yeshivah, Yeshivas Tomchei Temimim,* during the week of his wedding celebration. At that time, the Rebbe Rashab said, "By starting this *yeshivah...* I am kindling the lights which the Baal Shem Tov and the subsequent *Rebbeim* bequeathed to us, to fulfill the promise of spreading the wellsprings outward, to hasten the coming of the *Mashiach*" (*Sefer HaMaamarim* 5702, p. 133).

19. Although the translation of *Chassidus* into secular tongues reflects a descent from the original, the Previous Rebbe encouraged this step to amplify the efforts to spread the teachings of *Chassidus* outward and thus hasten the coming of *Mashiach.*

age (and the language in which the Baal Shem Tov and the *Rebbeim* which followed him would deliver *Chassidic* teachings), and spread these teachings into the seventy secular languages as well.[20]

Nevertheless, in these earlier generations (and even in the beginning of the Previous Rebbe's time) the fundamental emphasis was on spreading the wellsprings of *Chassidus* outward and not (as intensely) on the goal of this process — bringing *Mashiach*. It was known that the object of these endeavors was to bring *Mashiach*, and from time to time (e.g., during the *farbrengens* of *Yud Tes* [the 19th of] Kislev and the like) this was spoken about, but this purpose was not the focus of attention.

After the Previous Rebbe issued the call, "Immediately to *teshuvah*, immediately to Redemption" and continuing to the present day, by contrast, the emphasis has been placed on actually bringing *Mashiach* to the extent that every phase of our efforts in our Divine service (including the endeavors to spread the wellsprings of *Chassidus*) must be permeated with the intent to bring *Mashiach*. For this is the mission of our generation: to actually bring the Redemption.

Many decades have past since the time of the Previous Rebbe's announcement, "Immediately to *teshuvah*, immediately to Redemption," and the storm of activities initiated to bring *Mashiach*. Nevertheless, *Mashiach* has not yet come.

There is no explanation for this. Our Sages stated,[21] "All the appointed times for *Mashiach's* coming have already passed." Although they continued, "and the matter is dependent on *teshuvah* alone," surely we have already turned to G-d in *teshuvah*. Indeed, through a single thought of *teshuvah*, a person becomes transformed into a perfect

---

20. In this manner, not only Jews, but also gentiles have the potential to comprehend these spiritual concepts. Indeed, we can actually see this in the present day.

21. *Sanhedrin* 97b.

tzaddik.[22] And unquestionably, there is not a single Jew who has not had several thoughts of *teshuvah.*

What is there left to do? *Tehillim,* the Psalms of David, the [first] anointed king, we have said in abundance. *Farbrengens* have been held on numerous occasions. In spreading the wellsprings outward — for seven generations since the Baal Shem Tov — endeavors have been made, and they have enjoyed prodigious success. One might say that even greater efforts could be undertaken, so that these activities will be performed — to borrow a phrase from the liturgy[23] — "in accord with the commandments of Your will." But that is possible only as stated in that same prayer "there," in the *Beis HaMikdash.*

G-d only makes demands on an individual according to the potential he possesses.[24] And if indeed, G-d wants us to fulfill this service in a perfect way, let Him create the environment that will enable us to do so by bringing the Redemption. Afterwards, the Divine service of the Jews will surely be "in accord with the commandments of Your will," in consummate perfection.

And so, it is natural to ask: what can we do to bring *Mashiach* that has not already been done?

In reply, it is possible to suggest, as above, that the Divine service necessary is the expression of joy for the sake of bringing *Mashiach.*

Simchah breaks through barriers, including the barriers of exile. Moreover, *simchah* has a unique potential to bring about the Redemption. As explained in the series of discourses entitled *Samach Tisamach,*[25] although the phrase[26] "the day of the rejoicing of His heart" is interpreted as a reference to the building of the *Beis HaMikdash,*[27] during the

---

22. *Kiddushin* 49b (according to the text cited by the *Or Zerua*).
23. *Musaf* liturgy, *Siddur Tehillat HaShem,* p. 195.
24. C.f. *Midrash Tanchuma, Naso,* sec. 11.
25. *Sefer HaMaamarim 5657,* pgs. 233, 252.
26. *Shir HaShirim* 3:11.
27. See the conclusion of the tractate of *Taanis.*

First and Second *Batei HaMikdash*, G-d's happiness was not complete. It is only in the *Beis HaMikdash* to be built in the Era of the Redemption that there will be perfect happiness. "Then the happiness will reflect the essence of the *Ein Sof.*"

The *maamar* continues to explain that this essential joy can be aroused by the *simchah* experienced in connection with a *mitzvah*. Indeed, the *simchah* reaches higher than the *mitzvah* itself, precipitating the expression of the essential joy of the Era of the Redemption.

In the previous generations, people surely experienced *simchah* in connection with their observance of *mitzvos*. For the experience of this *simchah* is a fundamental element of Divine service as it is written,[28] "Serve G-d with happiness." Nevertheless, in previous generations, the emphasis was on the service of G-d, and that service was infused with happiness. The suggestion to use *simchah* as a catalyst to bring *Mashiach*, by contrast, puts the emphasis on the *simchah* itself, *simchah* in its pure and consummate state.

(Needless to say, for a Jew, even this pure expression of happiness must be connected with his Divine service in the Torah and its *mitzvos*, as it is written,[29] "The precepts of G-d are just, bringing joy to the heart." Nevertheless, the emphasis is on the *simchah* itself, not on the factors which bring it about. And this service of *simchah* should have as its goal — bringing *Mashiach*.)

One might ask: Why in the previous generations — especially after the Previous Rebbe's declaration "Immediately to Redemption" — was there not an emphasis on bringing *Mashiach* through *simchah*? Everything possible to bring *Mashiach* was done. To refer to the analogy cited previously, the precious jewel in the king's crown was pulverized so that it could be poured into the mouth of the king's son — indeed, the precious stone was spread into

---

28. *Tehillim* 100:2. See the explanation of this verse in the *Zohar*, Vol. III, p. 56a. See also the conclusion of *Hilchos Lulav* in the *Mishneh Torah*.
29. *Tehillim* 19:9.

seventy languages so that even a gentile could grasp it — and yet, there was no effort to bring *Mashiach* through *simchah*.

The resolution to this question is obvious. When the entire Jewish people — and the *Shechinah* — are found in the darkness of exile, the pain of exile prevents a pure and consummate expression of *simchah*.

Nevertheless, this should not hold us back from efforts in this direction, for ultimately, we must bring about the Redemption. And therefore the service of pure and consummate *simchah* is necessary. Moreover, the hardships of the exile should not create an impediment, for since this service is necessary to bring the Redemption, the potential is granted to experience such pure and consummate *simchah*.

This is within the grasp of every individual. By meditating on the imminence of *Mashiach's* coming and the knowledge that at that time, perfect *simchah* will spread throughout the entire world, it is possible to experience a microcosm of this *simchah* at present.

Indeed, the lengthy explanation of this concept is not in place, deed is what is most important. Announcements must be made about the importance of increasing *simchah* with the intent of bringing *Mashiach*. And if anyone questions the effectiveness of this proposal, let him put it to the test and he will see its effectiveness.

And this *simchah* will surely lead to the ultimate *simchah*, the rejoicing of the Redemption, when "then our mouths will be filled with joy."[30]

---

30. *Ibid.* 126:2.

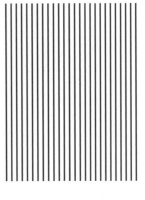

GLOSSARY

AriZal(lit., "the lion of blessed memory"): R. Isaac Luria (1534-1572), one of the leading Kabbalistic* luminaries

atzvus (lit. "sadness"): a heavy-hearted sense of depression

Beis HaMikdash: The Holy Temple in Jerusalem

bitochon (lit. "trust"): confidence in G-d's ever-present assistance

bittul: self-nullification; rising above one's personal concerns and dedicating one's energies towards a higher goal or level of awareness

b'simchah: in a state of joy

buttel: selfless, see *bittul*

Chabad (acronym for the Hebrew words meaning "wisdom, understanding, and knowledge"): the approach to *Chassidism* which filters its spiritual and emotional power through the intellect; a synonym for *Chabad* is *Lubavitch, the name of the town where this movement originally flourished

cheder, pl. *chedarim* (lit., "room"): Torah schools for young children

chassid (pl., *chassidim*): adherent of the *Chassidic* movement (see *Chassidus)

Chassidism: see *Chassidus

Chassidus: Chassidism, i.e., the movement within Orthodox Judaism founded in White Russia by R. Yisrael, the Baal Shem Tov (1698-1760), and stressing: emotional involvement in prayer; service of

G-d through the material universe; wholehearted earnestness in Divine service; the mystical in addition to the legalistic dimension of Judaism; the power of joy and of music; the love to be shown to *every* Jew, unconditionally; and the mutual physical and moral responsibility of the members of the informal *Chassidic* brotherhood, each *chassid* having cultivated a spiritual attachment to his saintly and charismatic leader, the *Rebbe; (b) the philosophy and literature of this movement; see also *Chabad*

Eretz Yisrael: the land of Israel

farbrengen: an informal gathering of *chassidim* for mutual edification and brotherly criticism

Gehinnom: purgatory

Hakkofos: the celebratory dancing with the Torah on Simchas Torah

hashgachah pratis: Divine Providence, the manner in which G-d controls every aspect of existence

holelus (lit. "frivolity"): happiness devoid of meaning or purpose

Kabbalah (lit., "received tradition"): the Jewish mystical tradition

kabbalas ol (lit., "the acceptance of [G-d's] yoke"): an unswerving, selfless commitment to carrying out the Will of G-d

kashrus: the state of being fit for use, a term most frequently used with regard to food

Kol Nidrei: the prayer recited before the evening service of Yom Kippur

Lubavitch: name of the village in White Russia which for a century was the home of the *Rebbeim* of *Chabad,* and which is hence used as a name for the movement

mashpia, pl. *mashpiim* (lit. "source of influence"): In *Chassidic* terminology, a spiritual mentor

matzah: the unleavened bread eaten on Passover

merirus (lit. "bitterness"): negative feelings which spur a person to positive activity

Midrash: the classical collections of the Sages' homiletical teachings on the Torah, on the non-literal level of *derush*

mikveh, pl. *mikvaos:* A ritual bath in which a person immerses himself as part of the transition from impurity to purity, or from a lower state of holiness to a higher state.

Mishnah: The fundamental compilation of the Oral Law compiled by Rabbi Yehudah HaNasi.

mitzvah (pl., *mitzvos*): a religious obligation; one of the 613 Commandments

nesi'im: leader; in the *Chassidic* context, synonymous with *Rebbe

nisayon: (lit. a "test") a challenge in one's Divine service

Olam HaBo (lit. "the world to come"): the spiritual realm of the souls in the afterlife; also used to refer to the Era of the Resurrection

Pirkei Avos: the Ethics of our Fathers, the tractate of the *Mishnah* which contains the ethical teachings of our Sages

Rambam (acronym for Rabbi Moshe ben Maimon; 1135-1204): Maimonides, one of the foremost Jewish thinkers of the Middle Ages; his *Mishneh Torah* is one of the pillars of Jewish law, and his *Guide to the Perplexed*, one of the classics of Jewish philosophy

Rebbe (lit., "my teacher [or master]"): saintly Torah leader who serves as spiritual guide to a following of *chassidim*

seder (lit., "order"): the order of service observed at home on the first two nights of Passover

Shabbos: the Sabbath

shul: synagogue

simchah: happiness, meaningful joy

Talmud: the basic compendium of Jewish law, thought, and Biblical commentary, comprising *Mishnah* and *Gemara;* when unspecified refers to the *Talmud Bavli,* the edition developed in Babylonia and edited at the end of the fifth century C.E.; the *Talmud Yerushalmi* is the edition compiled in *Eretz Yisrael* at the end of the fourth century C.E.

Tanya: the classic text of *Chabad Chassidic* thought authored by the Alter Rebbe

Tehillim: the Book of Psalms

teshuvah (lit., "return [to G-d]"): repentance

tzaddik (pl., *tzaddikim*): (a) completely righteous individual (b) *Rebbe

yesh (lit. "it exists") in *Chassidic* terminology, an entity which is limited and self-conscious

yeshivah, pl. *yeshivos:* Torah academy for advanced students

yetzer hora: the Evil Inclination

Zohar: (lit., "radiance"): classical work embodying the mystical teachings of the *Kabbalah*